CLASSROOM COMPUTERS

CLASSROOM COMPUTERS
A Practical Guide for Effective Teaching

Anthony C. Maffei, Ph.D.
Computer Coordinator
Piscataway, New Jersey

HUMAN SCIENCES PRESS, INC.
72 FIFTH AVENUE
NEW YORK, N.Y. 10011

Printed in the United States of America
987654321

Library of Congress Cataloging in Publication Data

Maffei, Anthony C.
  Classroom computers.

  Includes index.
    1. Computer-assisted instruction. 2. Education—
Computer programs. I. Title.
LB1028.5.M19   1986   371.3'9445   85-8206
ISBN 0-89885-251-X
ISBN 0-89885-255-2 (pbk.)

FOR MOM AND DAD—
WITH
AFFECTION AND ADMIRATION

CONTENTS

ACKNOWLEDGEMENTS

This book is a reflection of my teaching years. These experiences have shaped my ideas about teaching and what it ought to be. Consequently, I must thank all my former fellow educators and students for their direct and indirect input. Hang in there—things will get better!

Dr. Al Eads, Jr., principal of Gaffney High School, Gaffney, SC was instrumental in providing me with the needed equipment as well as some stimulating ideas; as was Sara Simons, biology teacher at St. John's High School, Darlington, SC.

The Darlington Public Schools, Darlington, SC were very helpful in letting me use their equipment and personnel in testing out my ideas.

The creative illustrations in this book by senior James O'Neal show a promising future.

Donna Nicholson hung in there to type the final, final draft!

And, of course, one must not forget Doris Barlow and her yawns of wisdom as well as the notorious five and bedtime, and finally peace and quiet!

PERMISSIONS

Chapter 4. (1) Reading Comprehension © Frank S. Toth, Jr. (2) © Scott, Foresman and Co. (3) © Tandy Corp. (4-6) same as 21-22 Chapter 3. (7) © Micro School Programs. (8) same as 21-22 Chapter 3. (9) MECC, St. Paul, MN, copyright 1981. (10) same as 21-22 Chapter 3. (11) © Concept Educational Software, Allentown, PA. (12) © Tandy Corp. (13) MECC, St. Paul, MN, copyright 1981. (14) © CUE/Soft-swap. (15) MECC, St. Paul, MN, copyright 1981. (16-18) © Tandy Corp. (19-21) © R. Eckert and *The Journal of Computers in Mathematics and Science Teaching*, Spring 1982. (22-24) © Tandy Corp. (25-26) © Broderbund Software Inc. and Scholastic Inc. (27-29) © Tandy Corp. (30) same as 21-22 Chapter 3. (31-33) MECC, St. Paul, MN, copyright 1981. (34) The Spanish Hangman © George Earl.

Chapter 5. (1) Apple and Silentype are registered trademarks of Apple Computer, Inc. (2-6) © Tandy Corp.; Darlington County Public Schools, Darlington, SC.

Chapter 6. (1) © Tandy Corp.; Darlington County Public Schools, Darlington, SC. (2-21) Author programs written on TRS-80 III and IV which are registered trademarks of Tandy Corp.

Chapter 7. (1) © Tandy Corp.; Darlington County Public Schools, Darlington, SC. (2-18) Author programs written on TRS-80 III and IV which are registered trademarks of Tandy Corp.

Chapter 8. (1-25) Author programs written on TRS-80 III and IV which are registered trademarks of Tandy Corp.

Chapter 9. (1-21) Author programs written on TI 99/4A (with TI Logo cartridge) which is a registered trademark of Texas Instruments.

Apple II, Apple II Plus, and Apple IIe are registered trademarks of Apple Computer, Inc.

ATARI is a registered trademark of Atari, Inc.

Commodore 64/VIC 20 are registered trademarks of Commodore Business Machines.

IBM PC is a registered trademark of International Business Machines, Inc.

TI 99/4A is a registered trademark of Texas Instruments.

TRS-80 I, III and IV are registered trademarks of Tandy Corporation.

PREFACE

The use of microcomputers in the classroom is a growing and exciting event. As with anything new, the emerging terminology can be quite confusing at times. CMI, CAI, BASIC, and RAM are just a few of the acronyms used to describe what computers are or what they can do. In order to lend some clarity to a possibly baffling situation, this book, written for teachers and future teachers, will adopt two roles for classroom computer use.

Part I will view computers as tools to help teachers teach their subject matter. Here already existing application programs "control" the users. These programs can be subject matter oriented, authoring systems where teachers prepare lessons and tests, or management software for doing grades.

Part II will view computers as being "controlled" by the user. Here simple and straightforward programming commands will be learned for doing small specific tasks. No suggestion is made that teachers need to be programmers. Many do not have the time nor desire. Rather, the emphasis is on learning those commands that place the user in charge and raise the question "why?" Such an attitude should be part of everyone's learning process!

With this distinction out of the way, terminology will be kept at a minimum and used only when appropriate.

Part I

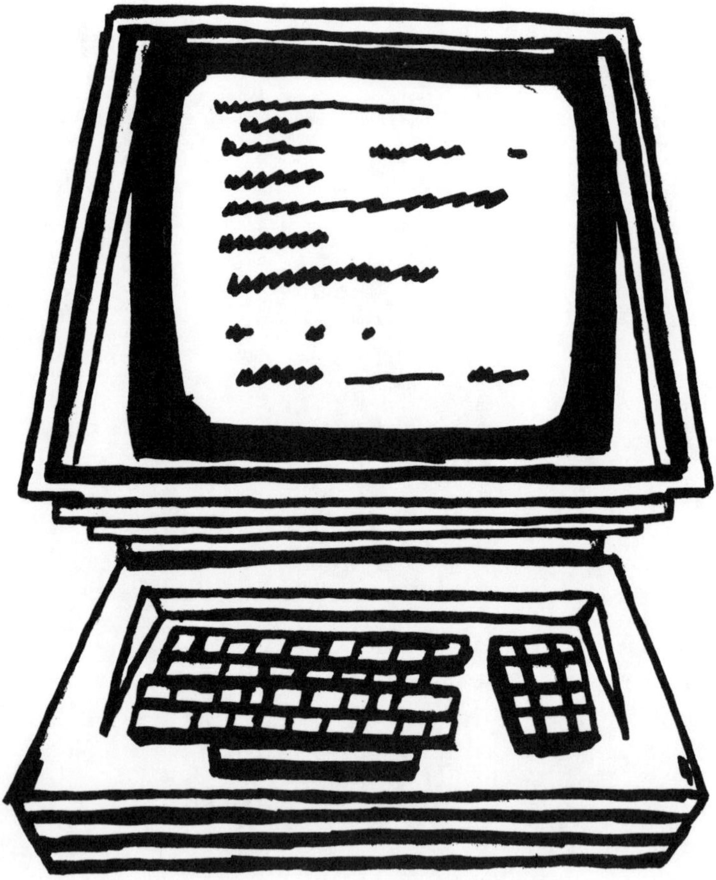

Chapter I

INTRODUCTION

AGE OF THE COMPUTER

The informational era is making its impact on the public schools as seen in the increasing purchase of the personal computer commonly known as the microcomputer or simply the computer. Unlike educational fads in the past that were here one day and gone the next, the push to purchase micros by the schools comes from many outside sources. One obvious influence is the business-industry sector. As many companies are becoming computerized they are indirectly placing pressure on the schools to train students who will be computer literate (a phrase, by the way, with as many interpretations as there are brand-name computers). Parents are also exerting their influence on the schools to have their sons and daughters prepared for our growing computerized society.

No doubt the schools face a tremendous amount of work ahead of them as they try to keep on top of a situation where they find themselves in a slight dilemma. Since the microcomputer phenomenon is only a few years old they face the task of educating their staff as they educate their students.

CURRENT USE

Surveys show that the schools are trying to keep their heads above water in meeting these demands. A study (*Electronic Learning*, 9/83) by Johns Hopkins University shows that at the elementary level most of the computers are'used in developing literacy skills (we are assuming this means computer terminology, some programming, computer usage in our society, etc). Some schools are also taking advantage of the speed and the effortless devotion of these quiet and obedient servants in drill and practice instruction. On the secondary level computers are used mostly to teach computer literacy skills and programming (mainly in BASIC).

The study also shows that a maximum number of elementary school children receive an average of 30 minutes of computer time per week. On the secondary level computer access is to a smaller number of students for about 45 minutes of computer time per week. Since the average amount of instructional time in today's schools is about 1500 minutes per school week per student, "on time" computer usage is very small for these students and nonexistent for many other students.

No doubt the cost of purchasing computers is a definite obstacle in having more students receive some form of computer training. It may be inferred from this survey that only a small handful of teachers from those schools with micros has volunteered or, even worse, has been appointed by the principal to take charge of the computer courses. This means that in a school with microcomputers many teachers are not using them at all!

However, let's imagine that there were enough computers in a school for each teacher. Would the average teacher seize the opportunity to use them? The answer to this interesting question brings us to the next topic.

CYBERPHOBIA

Fear of computers is by no means an experience faced only by the average classroom teacher. Many other people see the onslaught of these highly technological creatures as a threat to their power, their security, and ultimately their freedom. In a survey (Morris & Lumsden, 1984) administered to over 450 public school educators, more than 85 percent agreed that computers were valuable instruments that could be used to improve the quality of education. More than 80 percent also said that teachers should know how to use them in the classroom.

However, a significant difference arose between these two statements and the last one which registered how much desire there was on the part of the teacher to have a computer for use in the teacher's own classroom. Only a little over 66 percent wanted one for classroom use. This gap between the first two statements and the last suggests teacher concern over the fact that computers in the classroom will diminish their autonomy and just possibly some day will eliminate their position.

Teacher anxieties over computers in the classroom are very natural and well-grounded. I would not want my position as a teacher eventually eliminated because of one. In fact if I knew beforehand that this would be the intent of my administrators when they placed that order for the "special one" with artificial intelligence I would probably conclude that their district was not worth my time and leave for one that valued it.

Since teaching is essentially at its core a human-to-human endeavor, teacher replacement by a microcomputer is highly unlikely. What will probably happen is that the role of the teacher as sole dispenser of knowledge will be taken over in varying degrees by the personal computer. This will allow the teacher more time to work with students individually and in groups where computers cannot compete and will never be as good as humans at analyzing, synthesizing, and evaluating problems, events, and ideas. The potential widespread use of computers to aid teachers in the instructional process cannot happen at a better time. Teaching, once a prestigious profession, is decreasing in membership due to many factors.

INSTRUCTION AND ACHIEVEMENT

There are many direct and indirect problems plaguing the public school classroom and affecting student achievement. Discipline problems, drug use, low curriculum standards, inadequate financing, poor teaching, and lack of parental involvement are just a few of the problems that seem to be always making headlines. Many state governments in consultation with their education departments pass laws and enact reforms to address these problems. Local school boards and administrators make new policies that aim at improving the quality of instruction. Some of these policies and laws have some bearing on improving student performance but many well-intentioned rules and mandates lose their punch in the usual bureaucratic chain of command. They sometimes have very little influence on raising student achievement or interest and in some cases they may hurt it by creating paperwork for teachers which means less time for teacher preparation.

Most teachers would concur that his/her inability to motivate approximately 25 different personalities for a sustained period of time is a real problem with far-reaching consequences. Through no choosing of his own a teacher must face on a daily basis students with varying ability levels, different backgrounds and interests, and be expected to teach them. Years ago when life was less complex and there was support for the teacher by many outside the classroom this task might have been a little more practicable. In today's complex society of individual freedoms, federal and state guidelines, high divorce rates, and mobile families, motivating students to learn is even more of a challenge with many new teachers as well as seasoned veterans experiencing real difficulties.

WHY THE MICRO IN THE CLASSROOM?

First, the personal computer should not be viewed as a panacea for our educational problems. Classroom use of the computer will

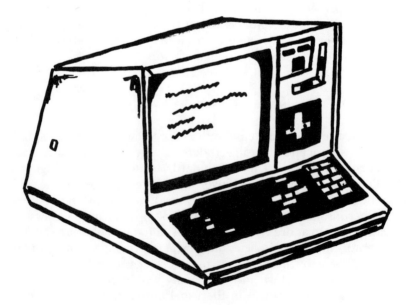

only be as good as the humans who plan well f
And since by nature humans have shortcomings,

One obvious and nonlimiting role of the compute.
room is to assist the teacher in the repetitive tasks of teaching ..
sics that are inherent in most all subject areas. Such tasks are time-
consuming and can be handled more efficiently by nonthreatening
machines. A more effective use of computers is to enhance the instructional process by allowing the teacher to present topics and ideas
in ways that in the past were limited by his imagination and resources.

Assuming that a well-organized district plan for the incorporation of personal computers into the classroom is made, student
achievement and teacher productivity should increase while teacher
inability to motivate students to learn should decrease. Consequently,
students will enjoy coming to school to learn and teachers, as well as
those outside, will develop more pride in a profession that deserves
such admiration.

The purpose of this book is to suggest to teachers and administrators ways in which classroom computers can contribute to achievement of this goal.

Chapter 2

CHALK, KEYBOARD, BLACKBOARD, CRT ... TOOLS OF THE TRADE

A COMPUTER SYSTEM

Rules and principles are created by people in order to give structure to the observable events around them. The purpose of this chapter is to examine such a similar principle when dealing with a computer system. It can be briefly and simply stated as: input yields output. There are many ways to input information to the computer. However, before input yields output, input data must first be processed by the computer.

Processing is done by the CPU or Central Processing Unit which physically consists of thousands of miniaturized circuits etched on a wafer-thin silicon chip about a half-inch square. The CPU resides on a main board inside the frame of the computer. Referred to as the "brains" of the computer system and commonly called a microprocessor, it sends incoming data to memory, works with numbers and logic, and controls other functions within the microcomputer.

A working knowledge of how to input and output data as well as an understanding of the terms relating to the CPU are essentials to the teaching process. Without getting too technical, we will briefly describe some of these important concepts that comprise a computer system.

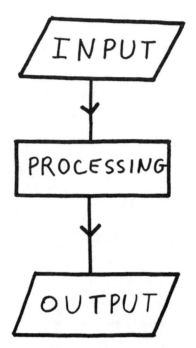

A CPU

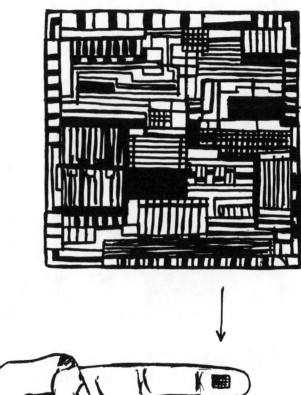

How to Input

We usually communicate with computers by means of a certain set of rules and procedures called a programming language (or software). The common ones used in the schools today are BASIC, Logo, and Pascal. We will show you later how to create from scratch your own little fun programs using some of these languages.

However, rather than write their own programs, most educators will purchase an application program that will meet a specific task in any of the content and/or management areas. For such software to be of any quality, it should be written by a team of programmers, curriculum designers, and subject matter specialists. It is quite possible that all these titles might be held by the same person. Now here are some of the ways teachers can input data to the CPU for processing:

1. The keyboard is currently the most common means in the schools of communicating instructions to a microprocessor. Since the keys are somewhat similar to a typewriter, it would be easier to input if one had some prior knowledge of their location. However, such knowledge is definitely not a prerequisite for operating a micro.

2. Voice recognition makes it possible for the user to communicate with the computer through the spoken word rather than the keyboard. It is an ideal mode of communication in those areas where the keyboard is impractical, such as with the handicapped.

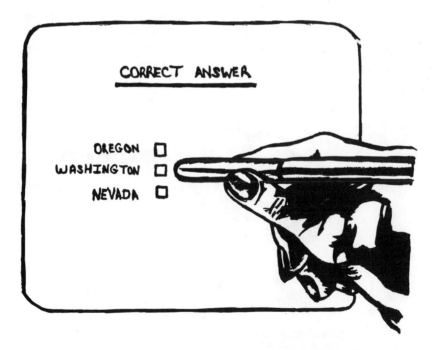

3. The light pen is attached by cable to the computer. It can be used to respond quickly to video inquiries without the need for keyboard searching. The tip of the pen emits light which is detected by way of the screen by an existing program in the computer's memory.

4. The mouse is one of the better innovations that allows for quick and effortless command of the computer. Movement on a flat surface of a small box that is wired to the computer permits one to position a pointer anywhere on the screen and choose from a list of options.

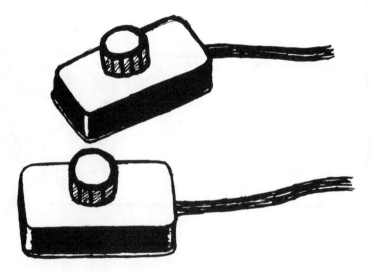

5. Paddles and joy sticks are other ways of controlling movement on the screen without the need of a keyboard. They are connected to the computer by cables and are often used in educational games.

6. Optical mark scanners are often used by teachers in scoring tests. The scanner can sense whether or not a mark is present on a paper form. Analyses of student grades can be tabulated by the computer.

7. Diskettes, cassettes, and cartridges are the most common means of communicating with the computer. Programs are stored on these input devices and are entered into the computer's memory by means of disk drives, cassette recorders, and cartridge slots, respectively. These input devices also serve as output which we will shortly look at.

THE CPU ENVIRONMENT

As already mentioned, the CPU is the center of control in the computer system. When we enter our input it goes directly to the central processing unit which reads our data in terms of bytes.

BYTES, RAM, AND ROM

A byte is equivalent to a letter (such as a P or an L, etc.), a number (1,2, or 3, etc.) or a neutral (such at the "#" symbol). However, our character "P" is not understood by the CPU as a "P" but is interpreted as a combination of 0's and 1's. Each character has its own unique configuration of just 0's and 1's known as the based two or binary number system. In comparison, our own number system uses ten digits (from 0 to 9) which is too long and awkward to be used by the computer for interpreting characters. Each 0 or 1 of an 8 byte combination is called a bit. Instead of reading eight bits at a time, some computers can read 16 or 32 bits. This means more speed in processing input since longer configurations of 0's and 1's are read at one time.

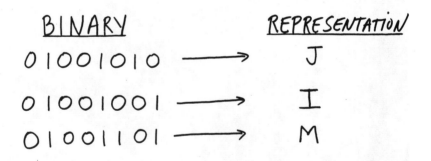

When the CPU first receives these combinations of 8 bits, they are physically stored in memory locations referred to as RAM (Random Access Memory). This data will be later processed by the CPU. RAM should not be confused with ROM (Read Only Memory) which is pre-programmed memory that comes with the computer and usually cannot be altered. ROM contains programs that allow you to communicate with the computer. For example, when you first turn on the computer ROM communicates either through BASIC or its operating system.

SPECIAL K's

Application programs are usually stored on cassettes, cartridges, and diskettes and then entered into RAM by the CPU. Programs come in different memory sizes and teachers need to know before they make a purchase that the size of their program does not exceed the memory capacity of their computer's RAM. Memory size is measured in terms of numbers of bytes. K is the symbol used to represent

1024 bytes. Consequently, 2K represents 2 times K or 2048 bytes and 48K represents 49,152 bytes of memory.

Most school computers have between 16K and 64K bytes of RAM. So, if your school purchases an application program which contains 32K bytes of information on a diskette and your school computer only has 16K bytes of RAM memory, you and your school have a slight problem! You can do one of two things: return the program and get your money back; or, if you can, increase the memory capacity of your RAM by having 16K or 32K more memory installed. When an application program meets the specificity of your computer's RAM you can then run your program safely and view the output—a term which we will now look at.

MODES OF OUTPUT

Output devices vary according to their purposes. There are several ways in which teachers can work with their output:

1. The screen or CRT (Cathode Ray Tube) is a video display that allows the user to view an application program. In one sense the CRT can be looked upon as an input device since we can see our commands on the screen before we send it to the CPU to be processed as output. Screens display characters both horizontally and vertically and the number across and down the screen depends upon the specifications of the particular micro brand.

2. A printer gives us a paper copy of whatever constitutes our output. The same output can usually be seen on the CRT. Printers vary in their types of output. Some can produce graphics as well as varying character sizes and styles.

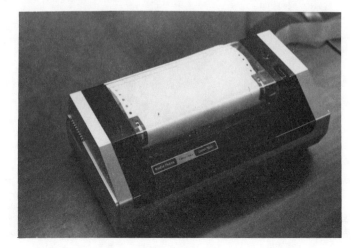

3. A voice synthesizer is attached to the computer and allows for speech output. Communication between the application program and the user by means of voice output makes the computer seem human. In turn, an application program could also accept voice as input turning the computer system into a "real live" classroom.

4. As well as serving as input, diskettes, cassettes, and cartridges can also be considered output devices. They can save responses to application programs as well as the program themselves.

As computer technology continues to improve, different ways of inputting, processing, and outputting data will emerge. However, this basic principle which underlies the computer system should always be recognizable.

```
THIS IS A SPELLING BEE
I WILL SHOW YOU A WORD FOR 5
SECONDS, THEN YOU MUST SPELL
IT BACK TO ME. AFTER 10 RIGHT
ANSWERS I WILL GO FASTER.
IF YOU GET 25 IN A ROW
YOU WIN


DO YOU WANT ME TO PICK THE WORDS
? yes
```

Chapter 3

INTEGRATING SOFTWARE INTO THE LESSON

PART A

Good Beginnings

Before we begin integrating software into the classroom lesson, teachers should be aware of classifications in instructional software. Certain programs stress drill and practice of the basic facts while others attempt to teach by placing the student in a learning situation that simulates the real thing.

Knowledge of types of software will help the teacher choose an appropriate application program to meet a specific objective. This is a prerequisite if computer instruction is to be introduced into the classroom in a systematic and structured fashion. Anything less stands the chance of relegating microcomputer instruction to the ghosts of educational fads of the past!

Types of Software

Classifying educational software according to its instructional type is not always a simple task. In some cases there will be overlapping. For example, a software package that is tutorial in nature might also include many drill and practice exercises. In any case, here are some basic distinctions:

1. Drill and practice software stress the learning of basic facts and skills. Almost all subjects in the K-12 curriculum require students to master, for example, dates in history, addition sentences, vocabulary definitions, scientific formulas, and the like. Knowledge of these facts and skills usually serves as the foundation for higher forms of learning, as in applying these skills and facts to a particular concrete situation. It would seem logical, therefore, that drill and practice software would be the main type of software used in the classroom. However, it should not be the only type of software used.

2. Tutorial software presents in sequential, incremental, and self-directing fashion a subject matter from its beginning to its end. The subject matter can be a topic in a unit, a unit itself, or a complete course. Through periodic testing which provides feedback, students are steered through the lesson. Tutorials are especially useful in classroom situations that are unable to meet the learning needs of specific types of students.

3. Simulations put students in situations that resemble what they are learning in class. Placed under certain conditions students are asked to make decisions based on available data. Use of simulations in the classroom provides students with an opportunity to learn when the real experience is impractical. In many cases simulations are presented to students unconvincingly by a combination of lecture, board work, discussion, textbook, or film. Consequently, simulation software offers teachers and students an exciting and new avenue to learning.

4. Problem solving should be at the heart of all curricula. Teaching problem solving techniques to students is also the most difficult process, for it involves several steps of which some or all can be applied to a variety of problems. At the present time there is very little software devoted to this important area. Learning a program language, such as BASIC or Logo, is a good start for experiencing a type of problem solving process.

5. Classroom management software basically can include a wide variety of programs involved in preparing and maintaining lessons and student records. It can consist of software written by a teacher to average student grades in any subject, a purchased drill and practice program which keeps track of a student's progress, or an authoring package that allows a teacher to create lessons and test-item banks. Any application software used to help reduce the continuous on-

slaught of teacher paperwork can fall under the heading of classroom management.

Choosing Software: Enhancing Our Way of Teaching

The quality of textbooks and workbooks varies from poor to excellent. The same applies to educational software. However, the reasons for selecting effective software are different from those in choosing textbooks and workbooks—our traditional media for instruction. We really do not want to use software where a textbook or any other mode of instruction is just as efficient. The cost factor alone would prohibit this. Rather, good software programs should pick up where other modes of instruction leave off or fall short. For example, in many cases it is impossible or impractical to bring the students to the learning experience. As educators we know that the best type of learning experience is when the student is actively involved with as many senses as possible in the learning process. Effective software can help in this. It can also help teachers keep track of a student's progress while instructing. And in certain cases software might redefine present curriculum and even create new areas in curriculum. Naturally, instructional software should always follow sound learning principles, be error-free in content, and show good curriculum design. With this in mind, here are some qualities one should look for when choosing educational software:

1. Are the directions for the student always clear and easy to follow with minimal teacher intervention? Some students have problems following oral as well as printed directions and the blame does not always rest with the student!

2. Is there immediate feedback to any incorrect response? Is the student also shown why her response is wrong? Given the typical hectic day of the classroom teacher this feat is just about impossible to perform for every student!

3. Do graphic designs or sound features enhance the learning process rather than distract from it?

4. Is the program highly motivational for the student? Getting students interested and involved in the learning process is perhaps the most difficult task facing the teacher today. Initial observations indicate a high degree of student interest in computer instruction. Given meaningful software, how long will this interest last?

5. Does the software provide a listing of students' progress in terms of objectives mastered?

6. Is the program free from content and grammatical error as well as from any asocial behavior?

7. Is the student actively involved in a program where she/he can select the learning rate, the types of problems, the level of difficulty, etc.?

It would probably be almost impossible to choose another mode of instruction that has the potential of satisfying all of the above conditions, except for computer instruction. And it seems obvious that by viewing current software, instruction by way of the micro is just barely touching the surface. It is up to the schools to support and use software meeting these specifications if they want to reduce classroom discipline problems, increase student interest in learning and in coming to school, and foster meaningful student interactions. The final note could also mean more respect inside and outside the teaching ranks for a profession that at this time could surely use it.

PART B

Preparing for the Lesson

Effective teaching of a topic in any content area requires the teacher to know the following: the general ability levels of the students, the teaching objectives to be met, and how these objectives will be pursued. These determinations form the basis of most lesson plans.

Computers can be used to reinforce, enrich, or introduce a topic in the subject areas. This means that the teacher must know how the software can be best employed to complement non-computer based instruction. In many cases, the application software will include reliable documentation (explanations and instructions) that will contain the components of a lesson plan for classroom implementation. However, a school district cannot depend on varying degrees of documentation or different forms of lesson plans which accompany the software. Instead, it should adopt its own standard lesson plan for each application program it possesses. This method will not only provide for a systematic approach on how application software can be used in the classroom but the lesson plan can also be used to include other relevant information.

For example, lesson plans for computer software should show how each program can provide for a smooth transition from computer instruction into other modes of instruction, such as group lecture or class discussion. Computer assisted instruction should not be the only mode of classroom instruction. If so, it will probably lead to monotony and eliminate other exciting and stimulating means such as the give-and-take of a classroom discussion, the techniques employed in teacher-guided discovery learning, or a description of the experiences of the real thing.

In developing standard lesson plans for instructional software, a school district will be setting up guidelines for teaching a topic. However, these lesson plans can only be developed successfully when administrators realize that teachers need the time to prepare them. Teachers cannot be expected to preview software and write a basic lesson plan during their preparation periods or after school. Sufficient freedom to think is not available at these times. One of the best periods is during the summer, for teachers who will be paid for their services.

Reviewing software and then preparing lessons will also give teachers the opportunity to share and discuss their ideas with each other. Such an endeavor has usually been undertaken in isolation and perhaps not as productively. Teachers need this time to exchange teaching ideas with their colleagues. When lessons are completed they can then be filed by content area, objective, or grade level, etc. and collated for all to use as a reference. In fact, a brief description of each plan can be stored on diskette by one of the many data base programs and then called up by a specific field such as content area or grade.

This systematic and structured preparation for computer instruction should in time lead to improving the entire teaching-learning process in terms of what, why, and how students will learn. Students, teachers, and administrators can then truly be accountable.

The Lesson Plan

Preparing a lesson for an application software program requires using a form which should incorporate this information:

1. Content area
2. Name of program
3. Grade/ability level
4. Type of software
5. Suggested group size
6. Brief description of software
7. Objectives of program
8. Integrating program into the lesson
9. District/state objective correlation

Note that the outline does not include an evaluation of the software in terms of appropriateness for class use. It is assumed that a committee of teachers, curriculum specialists, and administrators has already chosen the software for its incorporation into the classroom. The steps show only how the application program fits into the instructional and curricular setting.

Some Actual Lessons

The lesson plans that follow were written by "real live" teachers and administrators. The steps are self-explanatory:

I

1. *Content Area*: Language Arts: Alphabet
2. *Name of Program*: "Alphabet Antics"
3. *Grade/Ability Level*: First grade—all abilities
4. *Type of Software*: Drill and practice
5. *Suggested Group Size*: Individual, small group
6. *Brief Description of Software*: The purpose of this software is to reinforce, stabilize, or maintain the memory of letter sequences. This software will give the students extra practice and drill in the alphabetical order of letters.

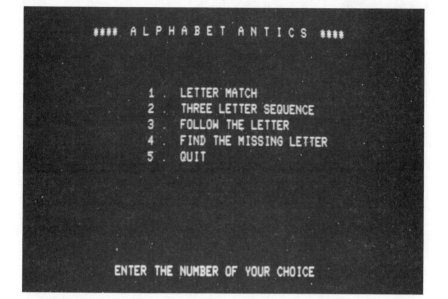

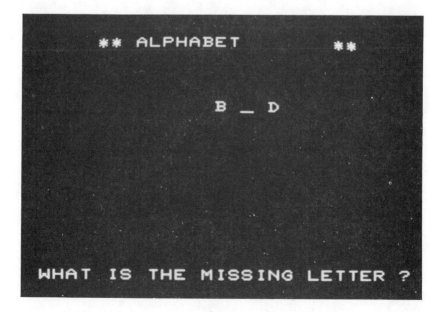

```
     ** ALPHABET          ,**


                 W M Y

NO, TERRY. TRY AGAIN.




      PRESS ANY KEY TO CONTINUE
```

7. *Objectives of Program*:
    (1) Students will be instructed to match the letters of the alphabet.
    (2) Students will be instructed to write the letter that follows the one shown.
    (3) Students will be instructed to fill in the middle letter of a three-letter alphabetical sequence.

8. *Integrating the Program into the Lesson*: Before using the software the students will have learned all the letters of the alphabet. They will be able to identify, recognize, and write the letters. This software can be followed with written activities that will reinforce the computer skills.

9. *District/State Objective Correlation*: District—Yes; State Basic Skills—Yes.

II

1. *Content Area*: Social Studies—General
2. *Name of Program*: "Oregon Trail"
3. *Grade/Ability Level*: 4–8, average
4. *Type of Software*: Simulation/problem solving
5. *Suggested Group Size*: Class and small group

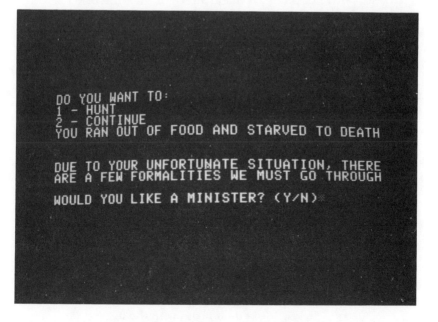

```
AFTER ALL YOUR PURCHASES YOU NOW HAVE
258 DOLLARS LEFT

MONDAY, MARCH 29, 1847

TOTAL MILEAGE IS 0 WITH 2040 TO GO

FOOD            BULLETS          CLOTHING
----            -------          --------

100             100              50

------------------------------------------

MISC. SUPP.     CASH
-----------     ----
90              258

PRESS <RETURN> TO CONTINUE....*
```

```
DO YOU WANT TO:
1 - HUNT
2 - CONTINUE
YOU RAN OUT OF FOOD AND STARVED TO DEATH

DUE TO YOUR UNFORTUNATE SITUATION, THERE
ARE A FEW FORMALITIES WE MUST GO THROUGH

WOULD YOU LIKE A MINISTER? (Y/N)*
```

6. *Brief Description of Software*: "Oregon Trail" simulates
a trip from Independence, Missouri to Oregon City,
Oregon taken by a family of five in 1847. The trip
covers 2040 miles and takes 5 or 6 months.

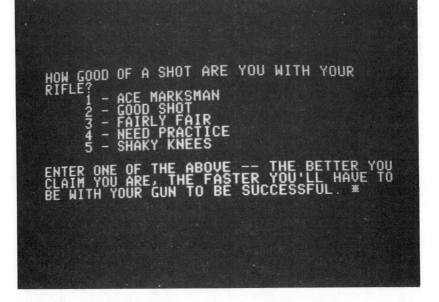

```
HOW GOOD OF A SHOT ARE YOU WITH YOUR
RIFLE?
        1 - ACE MARKSMAN
        2 - GOOD SHOT
        3 - FAIRLY FAIR
        4 - NEED PRACTICE
        5 - SHAKY KNEES

ENTER ONE OF THE ABOVE -- THE BETTER YOU
CLAIM YOU ARE, THE FASTER YOU'LL HAVE TO
BE WITH YOUR GUN TO BE SUCCESSFUL. ※
```

7. *Objectives of Program*:

   (1) The student is made aware of the difficulties encountered by early pioneers.

   (2) The student is required to make quick decisions that will determine whether or not the family survives the arduous journey.

   (3) The student learns to make the most of whatever resources he has at his disposal.

   (4) The student learns to manage a budget.

   (5) The student learns something about the geography of the northwest.

   (6) The student realizes the courage and ingenuity required of early pioneers.

8. *Integrating the Program into the Lesson*:

   (1)   Ideally, a class on the discovery of Oregon, early explorers, the influence and importance of fur trading, the "mountain men," and the influence of the missionaries should have already been conducted.

   The class could begin with the instructor telling the advantages such as rich soil and lucrative fur trading that attracted the settlers to Oregon. Wagon trains could be discussed—possible references could be made to the old TV series "Wagon Train."

(2)   At this point, the computer program "Oregon Trail" could be used. If enough computers were available, one or two students could be assigned to a computer. If not, the entire class could watch as a student went through the program.

(3)   To follow up, the class could recall the various obstacles faced by the settlers that were shown in the program.

Extra credit could be given to those who could go beyond the program and come up with additional problems.

The brightest students could attempt to determine what new national needs were created by the settling of the Oregon territory.

9. *District/State Objective Correlation*: NA

III

1. *Content Area*: General Science — Biology
2. *Name of Program*: "Fish"
3. *Grade/Ability Level*: 7–9
4. *Type of Software*: Tutorial
5. *Suggested Group Size*: Small group
6. *Brief Description of Software*: A tutorial on the circulatory system of animals which have two-chambered hearts, such as fish.
7. *Objectives of Program*:
   (1) To learn the route taken by blood in the circulatory system of two-chambered heart animals.
   (2) To recognize that oxygenated blood is carried to the parts of the body and unoxygenated blood is carried back to the heart.
   (3) To identify the chambers of a two-chambered heart.
8. *Integrating the Program into the Lesson*: Students should understand that blood functions to carry oxygenated

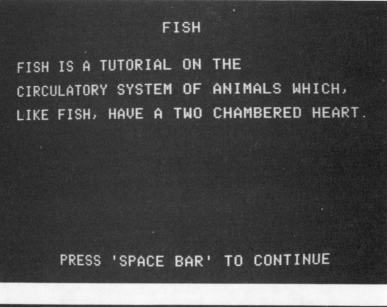

FISH

FISH IS A TUTORIAL ON THE
CIRCULATORY SYSTEM OF ANIMALS WHICH,
LIKE FISH, HAVE A TWO CHAMBERED HEART.

PRESS 'SPACE BAR' TO CONTINUE

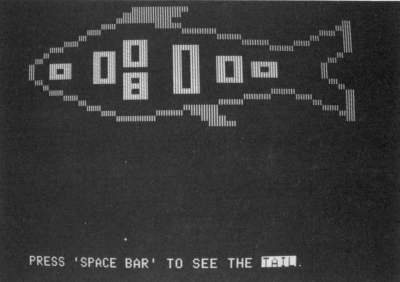

PRESS 'SPACE BAR' TO SEE THE TAIL.

blood to the blood cells and picks up unoxygenated blood and carries it to the heart. The heart works as a pump to move the blood through the circulatory system. General students should be able to use the program at one time. Worksheets can be used to reinforce what the computer has taught. Research other animals that have a two-chambered heart.

9. *District/State Objective Correlation*: Yes (Both)

IV

1. *Content Area*: Algebra—Graphing
2. *Name of Program*: "Graphs by Aladdin Software for Algebra Students"
3. *Grade/Ability Level*: Grades 9 through 12; above average
4. *Type of Software*: Drill and practice/demonstration
5. *Suggested Group Size*: Large (class)   or small groups
6. *Brief Description of Program*: The program demonstrates how equations of the form $Ax + By = C$ and $y = mx + b$ can be solved graphically. Students are prompted to practice with several equations.
7. *Objectives of Program:*
   (1) To graph equations of the type $Ax + By = C$
   (2) To graph equations of the type $y = mx + b$
   (3) To graph more than one equation at a time —type $y = mx + b$
   (4) To graph more than one equation at a time —type $Ax + By = C$
   (5) To graph linear inequalities

```
                    MENU

FOR SELECTION ENTER NUMBER AT LEFT

(1) TO GRAPH EQUATIONS OF THE TYPE  AX+BY=C
(2) TO GRAPH EQUATIONS OF THE TYPE  Y=MX+B
(3) TO GRAPH MORE THAN ONE EQUATION AT A TIME -- TYPE Y=MX+B
(4) TO GRAPH MORE THAN ONE EQUATION AT A TIME -- TYPE AX+BY=C
(5) TO GRAPH LINEAR INEQUALITIES


TO RETURN TO MENU ENTER '9' AT 'NEXT EQUATION' STATEMENT
```

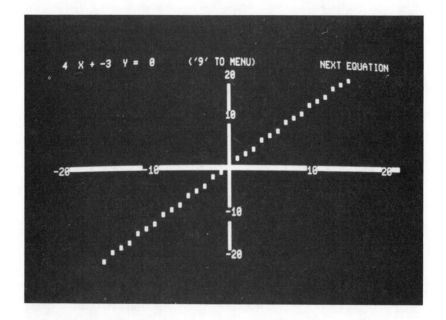

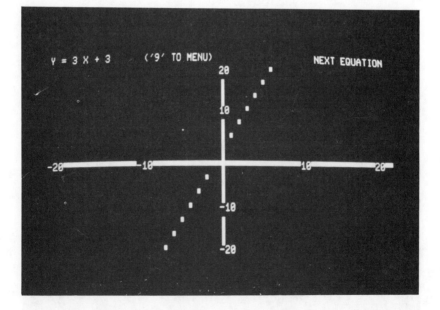

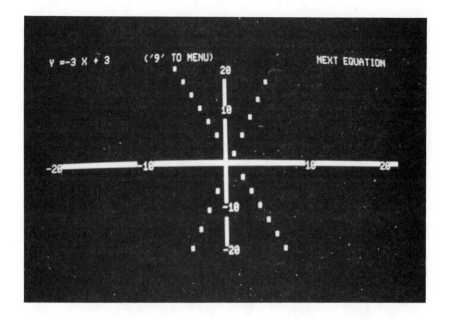

8. *Integrating the Program into the Lesson*: The key points
    of this program are illustrated through graphic solu-
    tions of linear equations and inequalities. This pro-
    gram can be used at different intervals in your lesson
    on graphs of linear equations. The flexibility allows
    you to review graphing more than one equation at
    a time. The program allows individual students to
    make up their own equations and to observe the
    graphic solution of these equations. This program
    generates its rectangular coordinate system.

    Students will work in pairs at the computer. Re-
    sults are to be recorded on the worksheet. Graph
    each equation using the computer to check your
    work. Indicate the (x) and (y) intercepts:

    (1) $x + 2 = y$ (2) $x = 2$

    (3) $3x - y = 9$ (4) $3x + 4y = 12$

    (5) $m = -5/6, b = 5/12$ (6) $m = 1, b = 4$

    (7) $m = 0, b = -5$

9. *District/State Objective Correlation*: Yes (Both)

V

1. *Content Area*: Business Math—Money

2. *Name of Program*: "Change Maker"

3. *Grade/Ability Level*: This program can be used in the ninth grade Business Math classes. The ability levels are from high to low.

4. *Type of Software*: Drill and practice

5. *Suggested Group Size*: Individual

6. *Brief Description of Software*: This is a drill and practice program on making correct change. The student is given the amount of the purchase and the amount the customer has given. He or she is then asked to give the amount of change broken down in pennies, nickels, dimes, quarters, 50-cent pieces, $1, $5, $10, and $20 bills.

7. *Objectives of Program:*

   (1) To give students more experience in change making.

   (2) To reinforce addition with different denominations of money.

8. *Integrating the Program into the Lesson*: This program will be used by the ninth grade Business Math classes. This program is an excellent drill and practice that will allow the students additional practice beyond the textbooks and workbooks. The outstanding feature is that the amounts the students give are tabulated on the screen so that they can see how each amount is building up to make the proper change. If the amount is incorrect they are given a choice: (1) Type 1 if you would like to try again; (2) Type 2 if you would like to see the answer. If there is a more efficient way to make the change they are given a choice: (1) Try this problem again; (2) See the other way to make the change; (3) Try another problem.

   Each student who is experiencing difficulty with textbook and workbook drill will be given time for drill and practice on this program. After all the students have completed adequate program drills, they

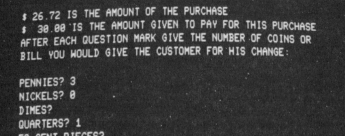

```
$ 26.72 IS THE AMOUNT OF THE PURCHASE
$ 30.00 IS THE AMOUNT GIVEN TO PAY FOR THIS PURCHASE
AFTER EACH QUESTION MARK GIVE THE NUMBER OF COINS OR
BILL YOU WOULD GIVE THE CUSTOMER FOR HIS CHANGE:


PENNIES? 3
NICKELS? 0
DIMES?
QUARTERS? 1
50-CENT PIECES?
$1 BILLS? 3
$5 BILLS?
$10 BILLS?
$20 BILLS?
GOOD !!  YOUR CHANGE IS CORRECT.
DO YOU WANT ANOTHER PROBLEM?
```

```
$  4.33 IS THE AMOUNT OF THE PURCHASE
$ 10.00 IS THE AMOUNT GIVEN TO PAY FOR THIS PURCHASE
AFTER EACH QUESTION MARK GIVE THE NUMBER OF COINS OR
BILL YOU WOULD GIVE THE CUSTOMER FOR HIS CHANGE:


PENNIES? 2
NICKELS? 2
DIMES?
```

will be given a written test on making change the most efficient way.

9. *District/State Objective Correlation*: Yes (Both)

VI

1. *Content Area*: Language Arts—Poetry
2. *Name of Program*: "Cinquain"
3. *Grade/Ability Level*: 9; average–accelerated
4. *Type of Software*: Tutorial
5. *Suggested Group Size*: 1 or 2 students per micro
6. *Brief Description of Software*: It defines a cinquain and provides instructions for writing one.
7. *Objectives of Program:*
   (1) To know what a cinquain is
   (2) To write a cinquain
   (3) To develop positive attitudes about this type of poetry
8. *Integrating the Program into the Lesson*:
   1. Introduction
       a. Discussion of what poetry is and is not.
       b. Reading of some modern poetry from textbooks and from books such as *Reflections on a Gift of Watermelon Pickle . . . and Other Modern Verse* by Stephen Dunning, Edward Lueders, and Hugh Smith, and *Over the Rim* by Tom Meschery.
       c. Listening to poetry in song lyrics by John Lennon, Paul McCartney, Bob Dylan, etc.
   2. Program—Cinquain
       Students now get an opportunity to write their own five-line poem as the computer gives them line-by-line instructions.
   3. Follow-up
       a. If they desire, students may share the cinquains they have written by reading them aloud, or they may illustrate and mount them for display on the classroom bulletin board.

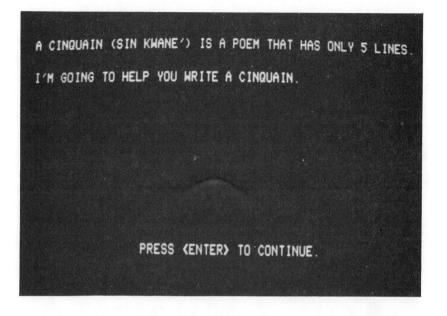

```
SUMMER

THAT'S THE FIRST LINE OF YOUR CINQUAIN.

THE SECOND LINE OF YOUR CINQUAIN NEEDS TWO WORDS THAT DESCRIBE
  SUMMER.

PLEASE TYPE IN A DESCRIPTION USING TWO WORDS.
? SUNNY WARM
```

```
CARSTEN, HERE IS YOUR CINQUAIN:



                    SUMMER

                  SUNNY WARM

                BEACH FUN WATER

          RELAX TAN TOM-COLLINS SWEAT

                    FALL

WOULD YOU LIKE TO TRY ANOTHER CINQUAIN?
(Y FOR YES OR .N FOR NO)=>
```

    b.   The best ones are then chosen by classmates and/or the teacher to be printed in a booklet containing poems written by the class to illustrate the types of poetry studied.

    c.   The students may now write additional five-line poems that do not have the seasons as the subject.

9.   *District/State Objective Correlation*: Yes (Both)

VII

1.   *Content Area*: Biology

2.   *Name of Program*: "The Human Heart"

3.   *Grade/Ability Level*: 7th–12th grades

4.   *Type of Software*: Drill and practice

5.   *Suggested Group Size*: Small groups/demonstration

6.   *Brief Description of Software*: To aid in understanding the parts of the heart, this program provides a drawing of the human heart. Letters are used to label the parts of the heart and the student is asked to identify

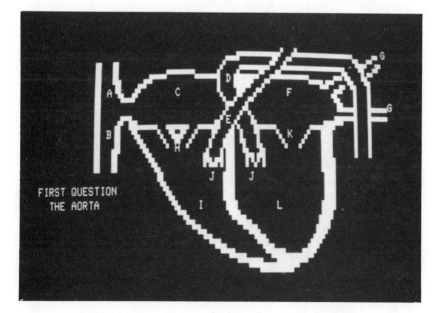

various parts. At the end of the program, the computer will tell the student how well he performed by letting him know how many questions he tried and how many he got correct.

7. *Objectives of Program*: Students are required to label parts of a human heart from a graphic representation.

8. *Integrating the Program into the Lesson*: The teacher should lecture beforehand on the anatomy of the human heart so that students will get an understanding of what the heart looks like.

   He will tell the class about the program that will be used to help reinforce what has been taught during the lecture. Students can then be assigned to the computer in small groups. Since the program takes only 10–12 minutes to run, all students in the class could get a chance to use the program during the class period. As students finish running the program, a worksheet will be used to find out if each can label the parts of the heart correctly.

9. *District/State Objective Correlation*: Yes (Both)

VIII

1. *Content Area*: Language Arts: Syllabicating

2. *Name of Program*: "Syllables"

3. *Grade/Ability Level*: Grades 7 and up

4. *Type of Software*: Drill and practice

5. *Suggested Group Size*: Small group

6. *Brief Description of Software*: This program gives a gamelike quality to the typically mundane activity of dividing words into syllables. It promotes self-competition with the use of a timer. Not only must a student try to divide the word correctly into syllables, he wants to do so as quickly as possible to beat his own record. At the end of the game, the computer lists all of the words the student missed so that he may record them on a syllable study sheet.

7. *Objectives of Program*:

   (1) Students are to divide words into syllables.

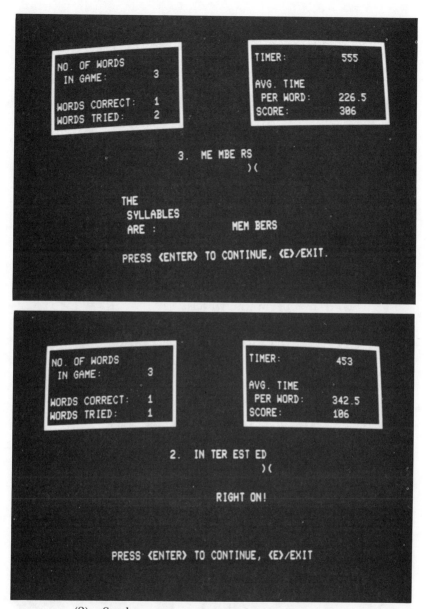

(2) Students are encouraged to beat their previous score in accuracy and timing.

8. *Integrating the Program into the Lesson*: The program can be used for remediation in the lower-level classroom and for a reward in college-prep or honors classes. Because it is a game, those students who are ahead in a unit would enjoy it and would profit from the review.

9. *District/State Objective Correlation*: Yes (Both)

IX

1. *Content Area*: Language Arts: Use of determiners
2. *Name of Program*: "A and An"
3. *Grade/Ability Level*: 3rd–5th grades
4. *Type of Software*: Drill and practice
5. *Suggested Group Size*: Three per terminal
6. *Brief Description of the Software*: The computer will show 10 sentences for the students. Each sentence will have a blank. The students will read each sentence and decide if "a" or "an" goes in the blank. They must remember that "a" goes before a word that begins with a consonant and "an" goes before words that begin with vowels.
7. *Objectives of Program*:
   (1) The students will be able to identify the common determiners "a" and "an."
   (2) The students will be able to identify determiners in given sentences.

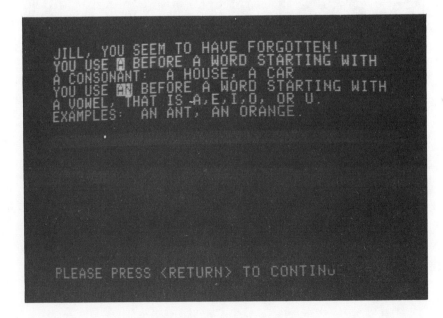

THEY LOST ___ ELEPHANT.

A OR AN?*

(3)   The student will be able to use the determiners "a" and "an" correctly.

8.   *Integrating the Program into the lesson*: Begin the lesson
by reviewing the two determiners "a" and "an." Then
write these words on the chalkboard: animal, owl, ea-
gle, deer, island, umpire, unit, honor, hammer, bear.
Ask a pupil to state whether each noun begins with a
vowel or with a consonant. Have volunteers write "a"
or "an" before each noun. Have others write on their
papers. After the completion of the lesson, the students are divided into groups doing several different
activities with the determiners. One group will be
working with the computer.

The software used to reinforce the lesson on "a"
and "an" is excellent for elementary students. Since
there are three students in the group, two will be
observing while one is actually working on the computer. As a follow-up, divide the class into two
groups. Have pupils in the first group give determiners. Have pupils in the second group respond by giving a noun that each determiner can introduce.

9.   *District/State Objective Correlation*: Both—None

X

1. *Content Area*: Typing I
2. *Name of Program*: "Typing"
3. *Grade/Ability Level*: 10th, 11th, and 12th (all students)
4. *Type of Software*: Drill and practice
5. *Suggested Group Size*: One
6. *Brief Description of Software*: This program could be considered remedial work for slow typing students or reinforcement for students who may immediately comprehend the typewriter keyboard. It is divided into three levels of typing: 1) beginners, 2) intermediate, and 3) advanced levels. The goal is to make each letter on the CRT disappear by striking the correct key on the keyboard.

   As the student progresses, he/she may move to a different level of difficulty. This time the student is still being drilled on accuracy and speed, but also the number of correct characters typed in the given time period. As the program ends, it gives the total number of words typed in the allowed time.

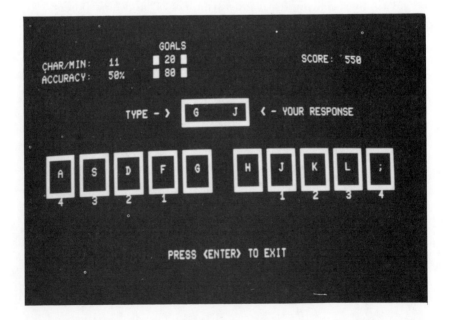

7. *Objectives of Program*:
   (1) The student will be able to place his/her hands in the correct typing position.
   (2) The student will learn the placement of all keys—letters, numbers, and characters.
   (3) The student will be able to practice on all keys on the computer keyboard.
   (4) The student will practice reducing errors on typewritten work.
   (5) The student will increase speed and accuracy on the keyboard.

8. *Integrating the Program Into the Lesson*: After the first few weeks of introducing the students to the typewriter, those students who need extra practice and reinforcement would be placed at the computer. Students who would like to improve accuracy would also be encouraged to practice on the computer.

   During a scheduled time the teacher would explain and demonstrate the use of the computer in business. Students can then take a series of very brief timed writings to see if their speed and accuracy have increased since practicing on the computer.

9. *District/State Objective Correlation*: District—Yes; State —NA

XI

1. *Content Area*: Mathematics: Fractions
2. *Name of Program*: "Fractions"
3. *Grade/Ability Level*: 3rd–5th grades
4. *Type of Software*: Tutorial/drill and practice
5. *Suggested Group Size*: Small groups
6. *Brief Description of Software*: This program gives the students a definition of fractions. It instructs them in identifying fractional parts of sets. It includes drill and practice and optional practice with story problems.

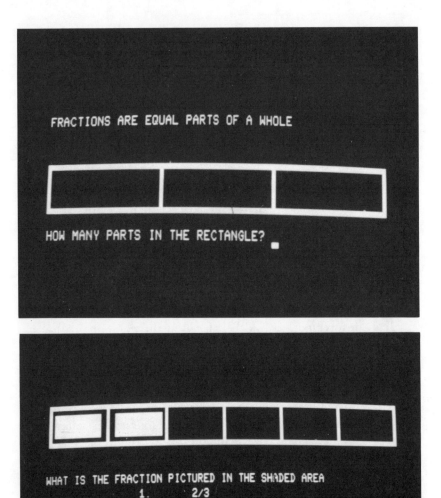

7. *Objectives of Program*:

   (1) Given a rectangle the student will be able to associate a fraction with the shaded area.

   (2) Given sets the students will be able to identify a fractional part of the set.

   (3) Students will be able to solve story problems where fractional numbers are used.

8. *Integrating the Program into the Lesson*: Introduce with a sheet of paper the concept of fractions as part of a whole. Have students fold the piece of paper in half. This would be repeated several times to generate other fractional numbers. Have students also shade parts of the folds.

    Then divide the class into pairs of students and demonstrate how to partition any set of objects. Each group should partition sets into halves, thirds, fourths, etc. Explain to class how the computer program on "Fractions" works. The students should go through the program and the teacher should give assistance when and where needed. For extension, all students should do follow-up worksheets.

9. *District/State Objectives Correlation*: Yes (Both)

XII

1. *Content Area*: Algebra II: Linear Equations
2. *Name of Program*: Teacher made

```
10 PRINT "INPUT A1, B1, C1"

20 INPUT A1, B1, C1

25 PRINT A1, B1, C1

30 PRINT "INPUT A2, B2, C2"

40 INPUT A2, B2, C2

45 PRINT A2, B2, C2

50 LET D = A1 * B2 - A2*B2

60 IF D = 0 THEN 110

70 LET X = (C1*B2-C2*B1)/D
```

```
80 LET Y = ( A1* C2-A2*C1)/D

90 PRINT "THE LINES INTERSECT AT
   (";X;",";Y;")."

100 END

110 IF A1 * C2 = A2 *C1 THEN 140

120 PRINT "THE LINES ARE PARALLEL"

130 END

140 PRINT "THE TWO EQUATIONS REPRESENT THE
    SAME LINE"

150 END
```

3. *Grade/Ability Level*: 10th–12th grades
4. *Type of Software*: Drill and practice/problem solving
5. *Suggested Group Size*: Small to large class
6. *Brief Description of the Software*: The program will decide if two linear equations intersect, are parallel, or are the same line when in the form:
$$a_1x + b_1y = c_1$$
$$a_2x + b_2y = c_2$$
Students will input the value of a, b, and c. The computer will then tell into which category the lines fall.
7. *Objectives of Program*:
   (1) Students will determine the relationship between 2 linear equations by using program.
   (2) Students will be able to predict the relationship of the equations by solving them algebraically and/or running program.
8. *Integrating the Program into the Lesson*: The teacher will demonstrate how to solve linear equations on the overhead projector or chalkboard. She will then introduce the program, explain the logic behind it, and

then demonstrate it. Students will run the program with some linear equations.

After gaining familiarity with the program, students can also be given equations where they are asked to predict if they are parallel, intersect, or are the same. They can test the predictions by running the program and/or solving them algebraically.

9. *District/State Objective Correlation*: Yes (Both)

XIII

1. *Content Area*: Computer Literacy—The Keyboard

2. *Name of Program*: "The Friendly Computer"

3. *Grade/Ability*: K-4

4. *Type of Software*: Tutorial/drill and practice

5. *Suggested Group Size*: One

6. *Brief Description of Software*: This program acquaints the student with the standard computer keyboard and provides for actual practice in locating keys.

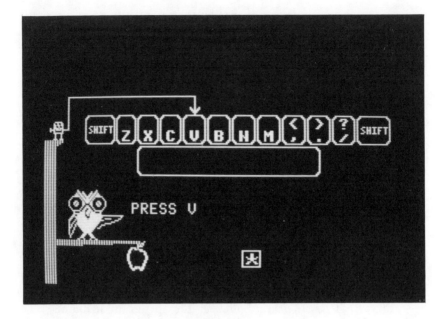

7. *Objectives of Program*:
    (1) The student will locate a key when prompted by an animated character.
    (2) The student will locate keys within a given time to test for speed and accuracy.

8. *Integrating the Program into the Lesson*: A large picture of a standard computer can be presented to the students. The teacher should go over the keys with a pointer. Students can be called up to the picture to locate certain keys. They can then be scheduled for individual hands-on practice at the computer for a period of at least 20 minutes each.

    Follow-up worksheets of computer keyboards can have students color-code with a circle those keys called out by a teacher or another student: for example, blue—K, red—T, brown—3, etc. A challenging activity might have several blank keys for the students to fill in.

9. *District/State Objective Correlation*: Yes (Both)

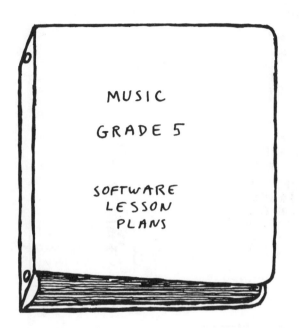

A Changing Curriculum

One interpretation of a curriculum is a set of goals, objectives, and activities devised to address needs. For those districts that already have an explicit set of objectives, activities, and goals, quality software will complement, enrich, and enhance this curriculum. For those districts that do not have such an established curriculum, the use of textbooks, workbooks, course outlines, and syllabi will constitute an implicit curriculum in which quality software will do the same. In both circumstances new needs will arise, for instance in the area of computer literacy where keyboarding, terminology, career applications, historical and social issues, and programming can also be addressed by applications software, lecture/discussion, textbooks/workbooks, field trips, and the like.

The lesson plans just presented attempt to provide teachers with some activities that will meet the implicit or explicit needs of a curriculum. They can be collected by grade/ability level and subject matter for teachers to use.

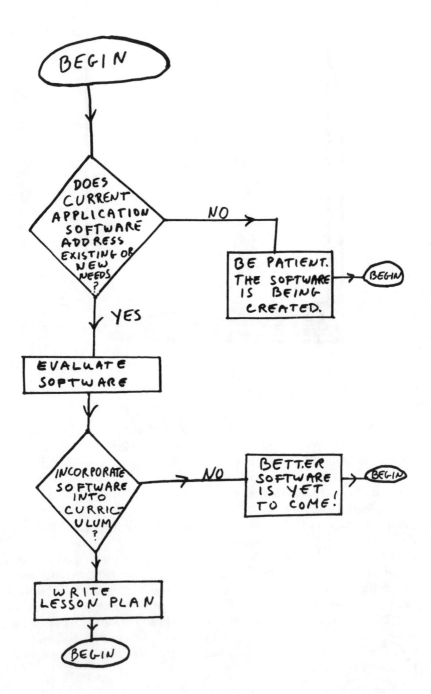

Quality software used to assist in the instruction of any subject matter should always address the range and depth of a curriculum as it contains novel, practical, and interesting ways of meeting a student's changing needs. In order for this curriculum to be effective in meeting these needs, ongoing evaluation of the application software is a necessity.

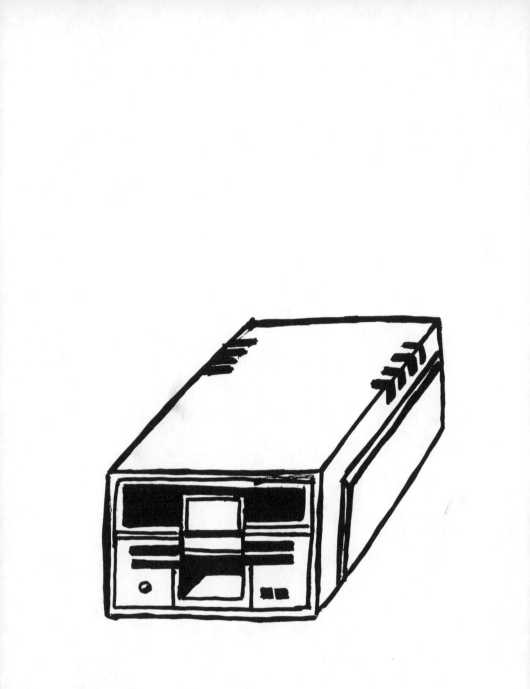

Chapter 4

MORE IDEAS
FOR THE CLASSROOM

WHY MICROS IN THE CLASSROOM?

Getting each student motivated to learn and to achieve according to her potential and on a regular sustained basis is a definite challenge for every classroom teacher. Obstacles in this path are discipline problems. Some of them can be attributed to an ineffective handling of the problem at the school level and/or a lack of support at home. Large class sizes, a weak set of curriculum standards, uninterested students, and inadequate teaching techniques are other factors that lower student motivation and consequently achievement.

No doubt there will be teachers who may not be convinced that computers in their subject areas could help them solve some of these problems. In fact, some teachers and administrators see teaching with computers as an impersonal intrusion on their ability to shape and determine a student's learning experiences. However, it is the belief offered here that it would be a mistake on the part of a teacher who, given the opportunity, did not utilize computers in his classroom.

Micros will not solve all the problems that raise obstacles to student achievement and teacher effectiveness. And, of course, there will always be the need for the personal touch of a caring and interested teacher to explain and elaborate upon an idea or to teach the higher thinking skills. Nonetheless, computers with the use of the appropriate software can definitely affect the attitudes of students towards learning and teachers toward teaching. The often overwhelming responsibility placed daily on the teacher for getting each student involved in the learning process will diminish to negotiable proportions with the use of micros.

Common sense, the classroom experience, and the capacity of the micro are the only evidence cited below as to why computers should be used in the classroom. Each area that will be discussed should not be viewed as distinct and separate from the next. Many of the ideas will overlap.

MEETING INDIVIDUAL NEEDS

In most classrooms one will find a gap in the performance levels among students. This means that in an elementary remedial reading class or in a high school honors geometry course there will be some students who are meeting the objectives of the course and some who are not, regardless of how aptly they have been placed in that course as a result of testing and teacher recommendations. But this should not be too much of a surprise, considering that we are all unique individuals with different learning styles, interests, intentions, and rates of development.

Most teachers recognize this fact and try to address the potential of each individual student. However, given an average class size of say 25 students this task hands a teacher perhaps his most difficult challenge! How can he meet and challenge the ability levels of students in his classroom, and keep his sanity? By himself, he can't. All that teachers can do is put forth their best effort. Much of this is in the form of extra help during and after class.

Some teachers ignore or give up on the problem of reaching the individual needs of students. Many teachers correctly blame a good deal of low student achievement on their poor study habits. However, the problem of how to reach each student still remains, even with students who do try and fail, and those who are underachievers. In some cases the profession receives an unfair amount of publicity about teachers unable to teach. However, many outside the classroom are really unaware of the obstacles that the average dedicated classroom teacher must face.

Computerized instruction offers the teacher the help that he needs. Computers have been used in the classroom before, but because of advances in technology have never enjoyed such a wide-

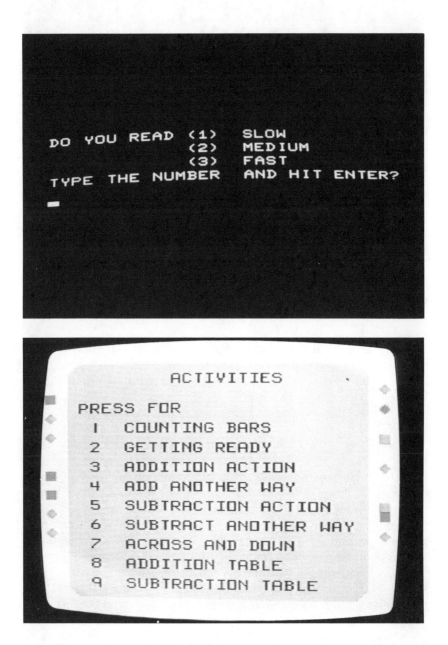

spread potential use. With minimal teacher intervention micros can in fact aid students at varying ability levels giving help to those who need it and presenting challenges to those who could use stimulation.

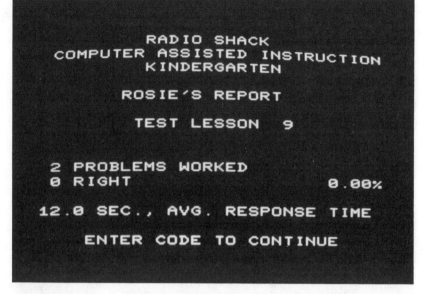

```
              RADIO SHACK
   COMPUTER ASSISTED INSTRUCTION
              KINDERGARTEN

           ROSIE'S REPORT

           TEST LESSON  9


   2 PROBLEMS WORKED
   0 RIGHT                        0.00%

   12.0 SEC., AVG. RESPONSE TIME

     ENTER CODE TO CONTINUE
```

Student progress can even be recorded on diskette, tape, the CRT, or the printer. This in itself is a definite aid for the teacher who is also constantly plagued with paperwork that saps her effectiveness in the classroom.

All these possibilities spell relief for teachers, especially for the conscientious and overworked ones, who have always tried to reach the potential of their students but until now have found it to be almost hopeless.

INVOLVING STUDENTS

Minimizing distractions and getting students involved in their classwork as efficiently and as quickly as possible should always be an important teacher goal. Much instructional time is wasted in the classroom quieting noisy students, responding to outside callers, taking attendance, listening to PA interruptions, handling student disruptions, and responding to noninstructional questions.

And even when a teacher can get all her students involved in a specific task without loss of time there is no guarantee that she has their minds on the task as well. A great deal of classroom instruction is wasted on those who give the appearance of doing, listening, and understanding. Nothing can be more frustrating to a teacher than to find how poorly some students did on an exam, quiz, or question after a great deal of teacher and supposed student preparation beforehand.

Compared with the passive learning that sometimes takes place in many classrooms, periodic computer learning should be a sought-after goal. Maintaining discipline would also be less of a problem as students settle down quickly to their personal computers and get ready to work.

INCREASING TEACHING IDEAS

Most teachers are always in search of new and motivating ways of teaching a particular topic. In many cases they are not in touch with such resources and, because of their hectic schedule, do not have the time to hunt for them on their own. Presenting a topic in varying ways is especially important to those students who do not understand the first or second way it was presented.

Employing as many senses in the teaching process as possible should be the instructional strategy of each teacher. Field trips, lab experiments, building blocks, paper folding, and measuring devices are just a few of the traditional techniques employed by teachers to get an idea across. When hands-on activities are not available, pictorial and graphic presentations of concepts by way of slides, film strips, instructional TV, the worksheet, chalkboard, and discussion are appropriate.

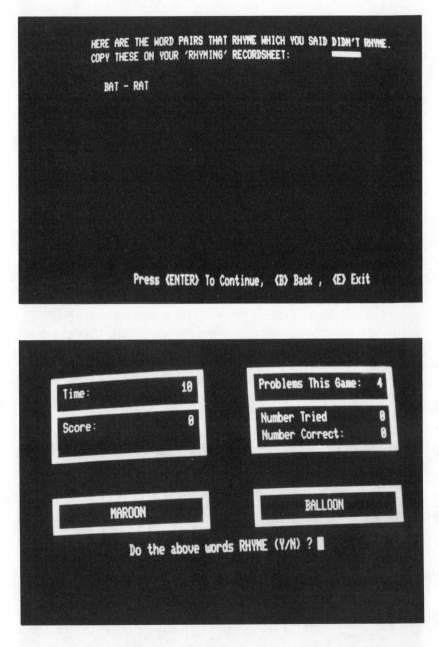

However, given a piece of quality software, students will be more involved in the learning process. Instruction by way of the micro is interactive, which means that students must get directly involved. Their micro keeps up a constant dialogue with them, informing them on the spot of their progress and consequently of a new direction they must take.

Teachers who do not use a variety of teaching resources tend to rely heavily on worksheets, workbooks, and textbook learning as the predominant mode of instruction. However, in the elementary and

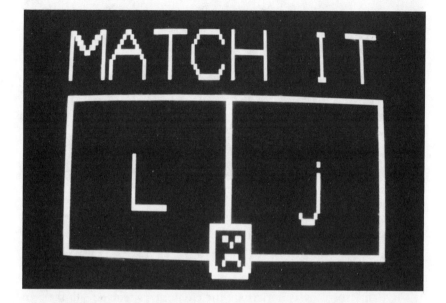

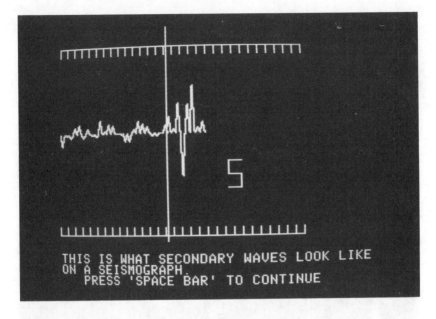

THIS IS WHAT SECONDARY WAVES LOOK LIKE
ON A SEISMOGRAPH.
PRESS 'SPACE BAR' TO CONTINUE

junior high grades students need as many different sensory and pictorial devices as possible to match their developmental growth and their impressionable minds. In the high school years, as the content level becomes more abstract, finding stimulating and interesting sensory and pictorial teaching devices becomes more difficult but no less important.

Quality software can increase the elementary teacher's limited arsenal of teaching ideas. On the high school level it can open possibili-

ED, THE ASSISTANT MANAGER,
              ^

WENT TO BUY GLOVES BATS

AND JELLY BEANS.

TYPE: <E> EXIT <D> LEFT <F> RIGHT
      <,> INSERT COMMA
      <X> DELETE COMMA
      <RETURN> SENTENCE COMPLETE

SENTENCES
THIS GAME: 3

NO. TRIED: 0
NO. CORRECT: 0

TIME: 174

AVG TIME PER
SENTENCE:

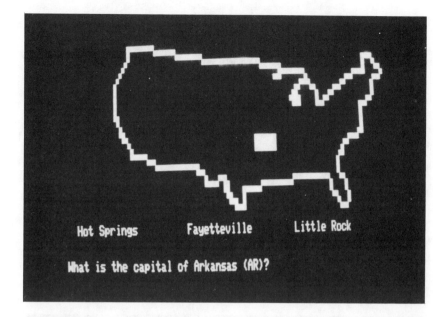

ties that until now the teacher never knew existed. Use of appropriate software will enrich the process of learning. Graphic designs, colorful models, appropriate nonvoice audio, pictorial displays, game formats, and animated drawings are just some of the ways topics can be introduced that were not available before. And, of course, the level of ability and rate of learning can be controlled by the teacher and/or student. Reinforcement is personal and immediate, as contrasted with the varying time it takes a teacher to grade and return a paper.

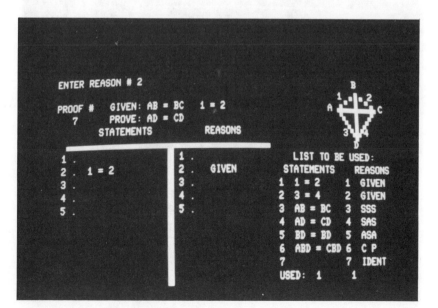

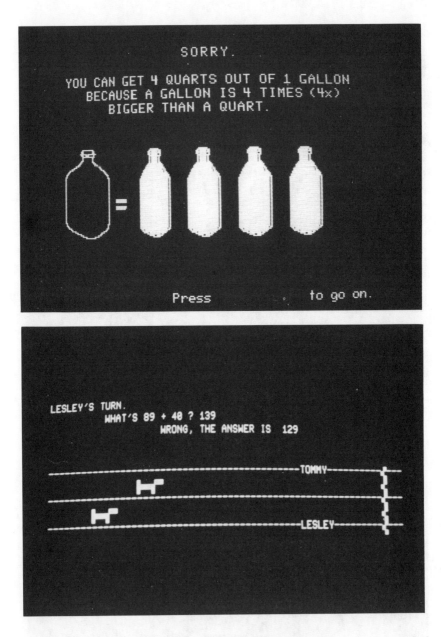

HELPING THE SPECIAL STUDENTS

Computer assisted instruction will probably have its greatest influence in meeting the diverse needs of the handicapped. Until a few years ago the handicapped student wasn't really a part of the public school scene. Recent federal legislation has changed this. It has brought the special student into the classroom, but not without the problems of how and what to teach him.

As with the regular student, the impact of computer instruction on the special student is still in transition as the state of the art in hardware and educational software development advances. One thing is certain; this growing technology is allowing those with special needs to communicate with the outside world instead of being tied to their handicap. Here are some of the things being done in the field of communication (refer to references for elaboration of these and other ideas in this section):

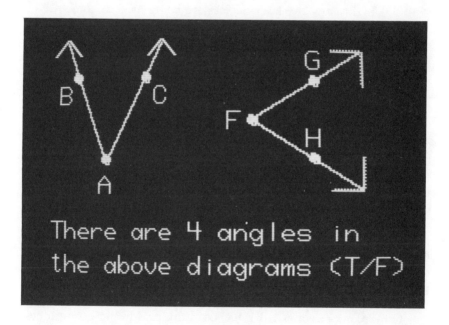

1. Computer software is providing distinct large print for those with learning problems or vision defects.

2. Those with oral communication problems are being helped with speech synthesizers.

3. Keyboard emulators allow those with limited movement to translate symbols into print or speech.

4. Computer programs are being developed to comprehend seemingly unintelligible speech and convert it to print or artificial speech.

5. Electronic bulletin board services offer the handicapped a chance to communicate with others.

6. All blind students will have access to any printed ma-
    terial through the use of a braille converter.

7. Special speech synthesizers can pronounce every-
    thing on the CRT for the severely visually impaired
    and the blind.

8. Children with difficulty in oral and written communi-
    cations are finding in the turtle graphic features of
    Logo a way of communicating and sharing ideas (see
    Chapter 9).

9. Light pens and laser devices are being used by some
    handicapped people to communicate with the non-
    handicapped.

10. Portable computers and telecommunication devices
    are being used by the deaf to communicate better
    with the outside world.

"Regular" software can also be used by a special student, especially the learning-disabled, when the rate and ability levels are controlled by the learner.

In addition to the above, compensating for sensory defects is another area of investigation that employs the technology of the microcomputer. Under development, for example, is the implanting of a
microprocessor in the ear of the seriously deaf. Auditory stimuli received by the processor are converted to impulses and sent to the
brain which interprets them as sound. A similar experiment is in process for the blind with electrodes that are first attached to a microcomputer and video camera and then implanted into the visual cortex of
the brain. This, so far, simulates vision.

Other compensatory work has been done with microcomputers
and microprocessors in the production of electronic arms, the electri-
cal stimulation of muscles, and the use of robots to perform tasks a
handicapped individual would find difficult. The microcomputer ex-
plosion is definitely out to touch and reach what once was an isolated
human being separated from society because of an affliction.

MANAGING THE SITUATION

One of the most unpleasant tasks faced by an educator is the
paperwork. Grading and filing tests, taking attendance, handing out
and collecting schedules and forms, filling out student progress reports, making up tests, responding to the constant flow of local and

state requests, and keeping on top of student records are just a sample of these nonteaching chores.

Unfortunately, we live in a society that is controlled by the proper form. The school system is no exception. However, the paperwork

```
   QUICK QUIZ OPTION LIST


   1    CREATE A FILE OF QUESTIONS
   2    RUN A TEST ALREADY ON FILE
   3    REVIEW AND EDIT A TEST ALREADY ON FILE
   4    REVIEW TEST RESULTS
   5    ERASE TEST RESULTS FROM DISKETTE
   6    PRINT OUT TEST ON LINE PRINTER
   7    END PROGRAM


   YOUR SELECTION:
```

```
       AM HIST    QUESTION 1    NAME: TOM F.
```

```
She wrote UNCLE TOM'S CABIN, a book and a play that caused many
people in the North to renew their antislavery demands

   1    Angela Grimke

   2    Dreda Scott

   3    Harriet B. Stowe

   4    Mrs.Daniel Webster
```

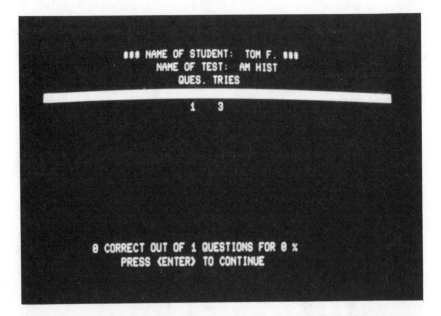

```
*** NAME OF STUDENT:   TOM F. ***
       NAME OF TEST:   AM HIST
            QUES. TRIES

             1    3




    0 CORRECT OUT OF 1 QUESTIONS FOR 0 %
         PRESS <ENTER> TO CONTINUE
```

crisis does take a teacher away from his primary function as an educator and the wise use of a micro will help the teacher manage his nonteaching activities more efficiently if he can find the time and motivation to learn how.

```
MENU

1   FILE NEW GRADES
2   SEE FILED GRADES FOR ENTIRE CLASS
3   CALCULATE FINAL AVERAGES
4   ENTER THE NAMES OF THE STUDENTS IN THE CLASS
5   CHANGE A FILED GRADE
6   SEE THE GRADES OF ONE STUDENT
7   CALCULATE THE AVERAGE OF ONE STUDENT
8   FINISH
SELECTION?  _
```

```
STUDENT #? 1

STUDENT # 1      CLARK EDDIE 9B

EXAMS           90  0  0  0  0
QUIZZES         70  0  0  0  0  0  0  0  0  0  0  0  0  0  0
LABS            90 100 95  0  0  0  0  0  0  0  0  0  0  0  0
  0
FINAL EXAM 0
FINAL AVERAGE 90
```

One of the best uses of a micro for teachers is in the area of generating test questions. Through appropriate software a teacher creates a variety of test items on a specific topic. He gives the answer key for each question to the computer and then a student sits at the

```
WEIGHT OF THE EXAMS (PERCENT)? 50
WEIGHT OF THE QUIZZES (PERCENT)? 10
WEIGHT OF THE LABS (PERCENT)? 10
WEIGHT OF THE FINAL EXAM? 30
HOW MANY EXAMS? 4
HOW MANY QUIZZES? 7
HOW MANY LABS? 5
MAXIMUM GRADE FOR QUIZZES? 100
MAXIMUM GRADE FOR LABS? 50
HOW MANY EXAMS WILL YOU ELIMINATE? 0
```

computer to take the test. Most software of this type will generate random test items on the topic or use a different form of the same test to keep the students honest. Results of each test are also saved on diskette or tape and in some cases specific content weaknesses are indicated to the student as a result of the test. In fact, software exists that will monitor the progress of a student's mastery of specific objectives or skills.

Another area of computer management is in grade recording. In many cases teachers assign different weights to homework, labs, quizzes, and tests. Homework might count 30 percent of a grade, quizzes 20 percent, and tests 50 percent. The software may offer the option of an individual printed report on the progress of each student. The report can be handed out to the student or posted on a bulletin board by student number. This is much easier than having them peering into your gradebook.

From the basic data, quarterly, semester, and final grades can be calculated. The eventual speed and accuracy of recording and keeping track of grades by way of micro should turn any computer skeptic into an ardent supporter.

Authoring software systems allow teachers to create their own lessons. This type of software permits the teacher to be independent of existing subject matter software and not worry about the need to

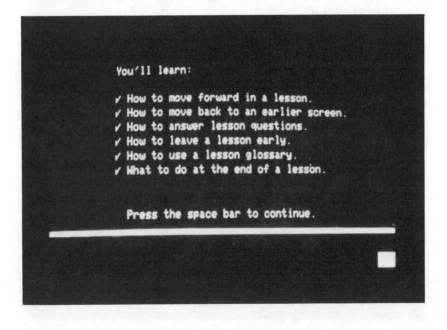

program. A good authoring system will include sample lessons for the teacher to follow. Usually a lesson first presents students with information. They are then asked questions about the information. Feedback is immediate and records of student grades can be maintained.

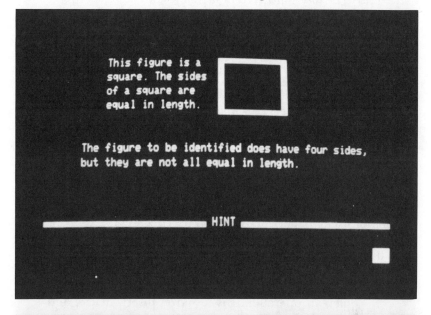

Management software is for teachers who desire efficiency when handling their numerical and non-numerical data. It is also for the teacher who feels trapped by the paperwork and would rather use the extra time to be more involved in his subject area.

Odds and Ends

There are many other areas which should attract any educator to using computers at their schools. Computer technology can touch upon almost every aspect of school life, with the promise of more efficient and more versatile uses to come. However, we must start our students in on it now and not wait for the computer or software to get better and/or cheaper. Such delay would not only put students behind other school districts who use them but it would also bypass the quality of some hardware and software. Here are just a few areas in which computers and quality software can make teaching more effective and/or doing paperwork less tedious:

1. Word processing software can be used in any classroom or activity where writing skills are emphasized. Writing becomes less painful as students learn how quick an operation it is to move, insert, delete, and

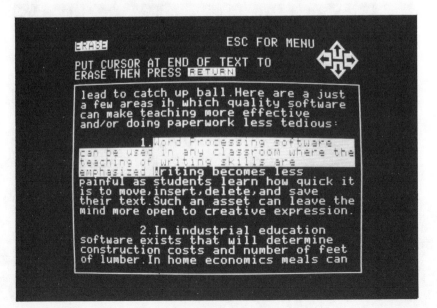

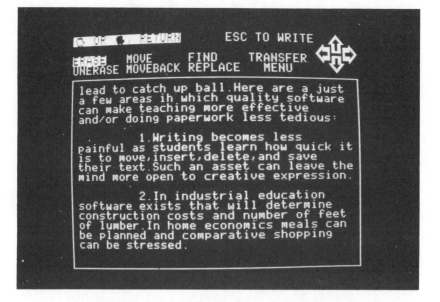

save their text. Such an asset makes revisions less of a chore and can free the mind for more creative expression.

2. In industrial education, software exists that will determine construction costs and the number of feet of lumber needed to do a job. In home economics, meals can be planned and comparative shopping stressed. Crop yields and soil erosion software are available in

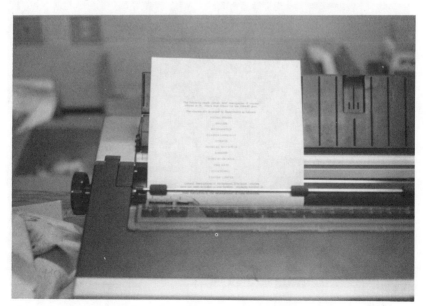

an agriculture class. The graphic arts class can use an appropriate word processing package to help with the layout and typing of the school newspaper.

3. Software can be purchased to determine the readability of texts, thereby ascertaining if it's the text affecting student achievement, or some other variable.

4. All school personnel need to keep records and/or lists. These consist typically of overdue books, the software and hardware in each school or district, failing students, attitude surveys, Individual Education Plans (IEP), AV equipment, and so forth. When these records and lists get long and need constant updating, an appropriate file management software system that adds, deletes, sorts, and selects information may be more efficient than working with the typewriter or doing it by hand.

5. Librarians will profit from software that manages the card catalog system, keeps statistics on monthly circulation, prints out overdue notices and fines, and even tests students on their library skills.

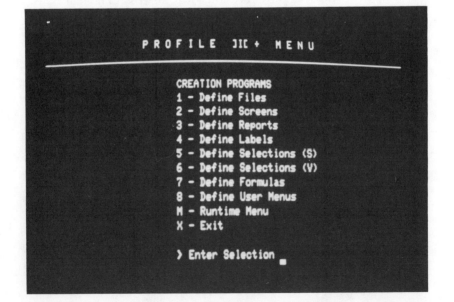

6. In sports, coaches can quickly keep track of various aspects of a player's statistics in baseball, football, basketball, bowling, or golf.

```
LAST NAME:BROWN              FIRST:HARVEY
GRADE: 5            TEACHER:STILLS
TEST DATE:3-12-83              SCHOOL:HOPKINS
VOCABULARY:67
COMPREHENSION:89
TOTAL READING:79
COMPUTATION:56
CONCEPTS:67
APPLICATIONS:34
TOTAL MATHEMATICS:59


#   2 D-Delete,  H-Hardcopy,  U-Updte,  X-End,  ENTER-Next
```

```
572.4  Bowman, John Stewart, 1931-        TIME:
B684       The Quest For Atlantis.            129
        Doubleday,1971.                    AVG. TIME
           182p.   illus., maps.              64
                                           SCORE:
                                              72

CORRECT, ALFRED!
            2. What type of card is this ? 2
                1. Title Card
                2. Author Card
                3. Subject Card

        PRESS <ENTER> TO CONTINUE, OR <E> EXIT
```

7. In addition to accessing data banks for job descriptions and opportunities, guidance departments can purchase software that helps students determine their interests, develops interview techniques, and provides job counseling.

8. By connecting a micro with a modem and telephone, data bases can be accessed that will give a student information on a topic in a subject area.

9. Spreadsheet software can be used in subjects such as history, science, or math where predictions based on observable data can be tested.

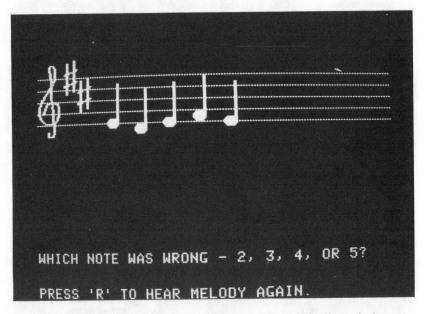

10. Art teachers will find software that will allow their students to generate easily varying art forms. Music teachers can train their students to be better listeners and/or composers.

11. Computer literacy courses are new and very suitable subjects for the micro.

12. Foreign language skills can be reviewed in a game format.

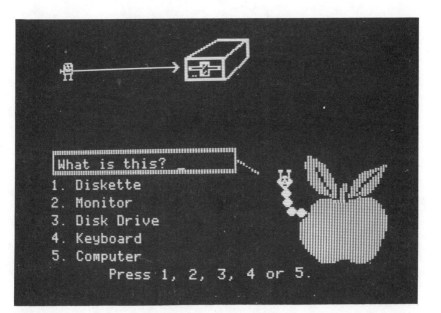

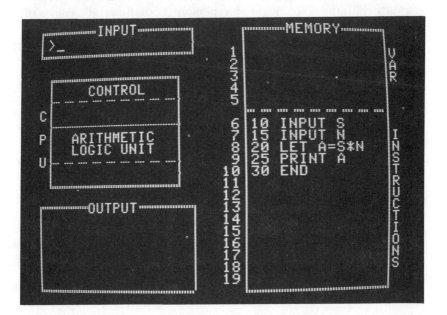

One word of warning should be mentioned when using software. Directions accompanying the software are not always as easy to follow as indicated in the ad or by the salesperson. Too often the creators of the software assume that the user knows what they know.

Software directions or any other types of documentation need to be read carefully and slowly. If they do not make sense to the user or things are not happening the way they should, it's probably the fault of the producer rather than the user. Vendors must strive to make their instructions intelligible, clear, and encouraging.

CHANGING DIRECTIONS

Computer instruction has the potential for not only making teaching less frustrating, more efficient, and more exciting but also for reshaping the curriculum. For example, it is quite conceivable that all mundane drill and practice can be taken over by nonintimidating, more appropriate, and more challenging computer software. This will free the teacher to work in the interesting and needed areas of developing thinking skills in children according to the potential of their developmental level.

Nurturing problem solving skills in children has always been a neglected area in the schools. Too often teachers tend to spend their teaching time on the basics, such as dates to be memorized, number facts, and vocabulary definitions, leaving little for comprehension, application, and analytical type problems. What happens is that we keep producing students who for the most part can only operate on this rote level. Developing the basic rote skills in each student is important because they serve as stepping stones to the higher, more challenging thinking skills. However, the basic skills should not be considered teaching ends in themselves.

Proper use of computerized instruction will allow the teacher the time to get into the higher cognitive domains of learning. It is unfortunate, but we tend to categorize, place, and consequently to teach students as a result of their standardized tests. We rarely have the time to take any student beyond the level of ability indicated by those tests.

Computerized instruction should free the teacher to develop ideas and techniques for reaching every student. And it will not be long before a range of quality software will assist teachers with ideas even in this area!

Chapter 5

ARRANGING THE CLASSROOM

THE DILEMMA

Meaningful and sound educational programs have often failed to get out of the closet and into operation because of a lack of know-how. In the case of micros, the problem is essentially the same. Where and how will they be placed so that everyone, and not only a couple of teachers, will have a fair chance of using them? The logistics of implementing an idea can be just as important as the idea itself.

HOW MANY COMPUTERS?

An obvious answer to the computer availability problem is for every teacher to have at least one computer in her classroom. The optimal and probably unachievable end for most schools is to have one computer for every two students. Unfortunately, there are many schools that possess a very limited number of computers and there are others barely able to afford just one or two. Public education is a reflection of our own economic structure and the problem of equity in school funding still remains. In the meantime, many resourceful administrators, teachers, parents, and students have been able to raise extra revenue for the purchase of computers and software through such diverse means as bake sales, soda machines, carnivals, or adopt-a-school programs sponsored by the business sector. The bottom line seems to be that if the desire and need to purchase micros is strong enough the source of funding will be available.

Distributing the Wealth

1. Computers to the Students

A problem arises when there are fewer computers than there are teachers. How can all teachers share equally in their use? In this situation a possible solution is to rotate the computers to a teacher's classroom on a regularly scheduled basis. The best way to achieve this is to place the computer on a cart or desk that can be wheeled.

The computer can be checked out for a whole day starting early in the morning or after class the previous day by the assigned teacher. An appropriate checkout point could be the media center or the principal's office. Teachers who must move from class to class may assign a capable student to help them transport the computer. However, the more a teacher's class schedule requires him to move around, the more difficult this type of arrangement. It would be ideal if a teacher could stay in an assigned class for at least half of the school day.

A typical school schedule might look like this:

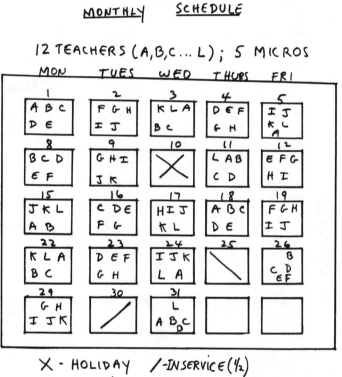

MONTHLY   SCHEDULE

12 TEACHERS (A,B,C...L); 5 MICROS

MON	TUES	WED	THURS	FRI
1	2	3	4	5
A B C D E	F G H I J	K L A B C	D E F G H	I J K L A
8	9	10	11	12
B C D E F	G H I J K	✕	L A B C D	E F G H I
15	16	17	18	19
J K L A B	C D E F G	H I J K L	A B C D E	F G H I J
22	23	24	25	26
K L A B C	D E F G H	I J K L A	╲	B C D E F
29	30	31		
G H I J K	╱	L A B C D		

✕ - HOLIDAY   ╱ - INSERVICE (½)
╲ - TESTING

Naturally the more computers a school has the more on-time for teachers and students. Given the above schedule, many teachers will have access to a computer for at least 2 full days of a week. Teachers who do not have any desire to use computers in their classroom (by now we hope that this number is approaching zero) will increase the computer time ratio for other teachers. Similar schedules can be made for schools whose computers number fewer than their teachers. At the end of the school day the assigned teacher or a responsible student would return the computer to its point of origin for the next teacher to use.

In the Classroom

When a teacher has a micro for a day he can utilize two basic classroom arrangements. Each one will depend on the type of instruction to be employed for a given topic. If a specific topic is to be presented to the whole class then a computer can be connected to a large monitor or TV and placed in front of the room for everyone to see while the teacher discusses the program with the students:

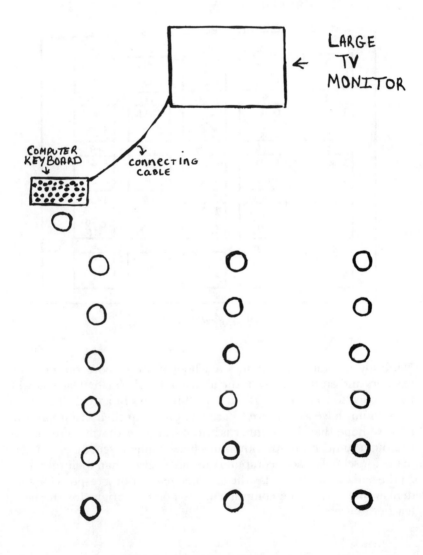

On the other hand, if the teacher wants to individualize instruction for a particular student or group of students, then the computer could be rolled to a specific part of the classroom for such study:

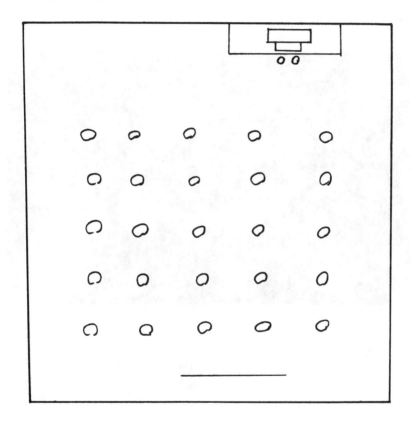

Here time at the computer can be scheduled for at least 20 minutes for no more than two students at a time.

2. Students to Computers

Another alternative to "sharing the wealth" is to establish a computer lab or resource room where both teachers and students travel to the computers:

Such an arrangement will require a daily schedule so that participating teachers and students can benefit fairly from such instruction:

COMPUTER
LAB SCHEDULE
15 TEACHERS (A, B, C ... O)

MON	TUE	WED	THURS	FRI
1 A	2 B	3 C	4 D	5 E
8 F	9 G	10 H	11 I	12 J
15 K	16 L	17 M	18 N	19 O
22 A	23 B	24 X	25 C	26 D
29 E	30 F	31 G		

X - HOLIDAY

Computers can be placed on tables in the center of the room allowing for lectures/discussions if desired:

Probably the most cost-effective way of using computers in a lab setting is through a network system.

The concept of such a system allows for a non-disk drive student computer to be linked by cable to a main micro or network box with at least two disk drives or a hard disk drive. Student programs can be loaded from or saved at the main drives. One version of a network system is to have cables from each student computer connected to a network box which in turn is connected to the main computer:

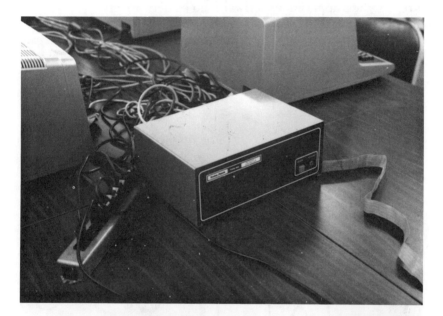

Some types of networking allow a teacher to review a student's work while still at the main computer. Printers can also be employed in networking. Students can work on individual or class assignments in a network setting. Those who adopt a network system should make sure that their applications software can be networked!

Besides the lab-resource room arrangement, there are other student-and-teacher-to-computer variations. Designated classrooms can be partitioned so that students can work at several computers on one side while other students can be working with the teacher at another end of the classroom:

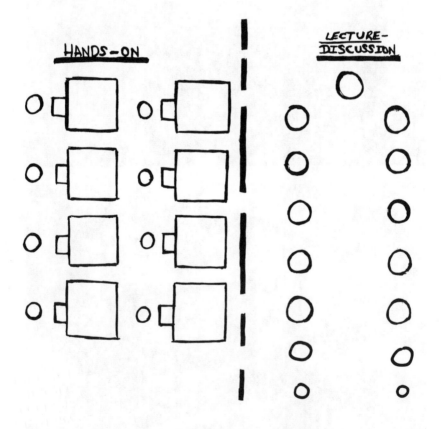

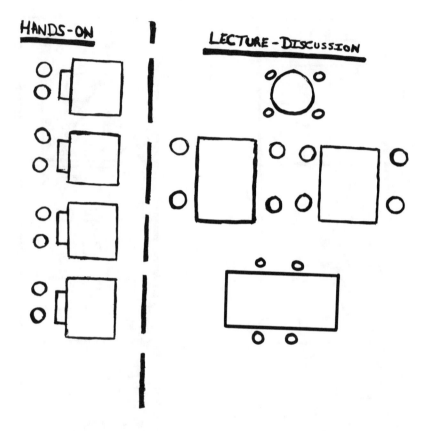

To Each His Own

The successful arrangement of micros will depend to a large degree on the preferences of teachers and principal, as well as on the availability of space. Apart from these variables, a little creativity and a good deal of initial work will be required to get a program off and then operating smoothly. In many cases, schools will calculate a combination of factors to meet the range of their instructional and managerial needs:

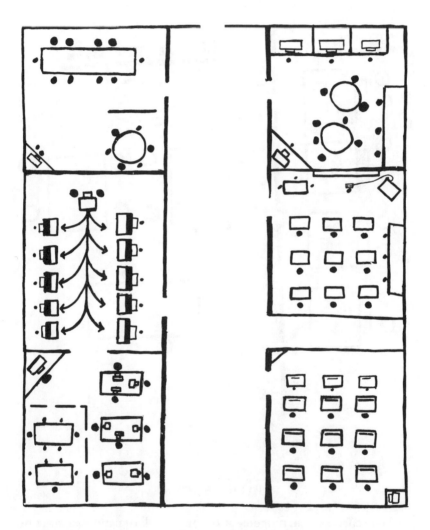

Schools should definitely steer away from installing computers in places that are out of a teacher's easy reach. This approach fails to acknowledge the teacher as the key person in implementing computer instruction.

Part II

Chapter 6

TAKING CHARGE
Learning Basic Commands

A Sense of Power

Teachers tend to encourage in their students a questioning attitude on the how, why, and what of things happening. Such thinking imparts the feeling of being in control of a situation and of comprehending causes for events. This is usually not the case when we use an application software package. In such an environment learners and teachers must follow the rules and regulations of the program which usually don't permit too much independent thinking. Of course, this is to be expected since we use a software package to achieve a particular learning outcome.

However, there will be times when it will be necessary to be in charge of doing or creating one's own "thing" as a part of the learning process. It is for this reason that we include some BASIC commands. BASIC is an acronym which stands for Beginners All-purpose Symbolic Instructional Code. Many instructional programs are written in BASIC, a language that is understood by almost all micros.

A Word of Warning

The reason for presenting BASIC is not so that you will become a programmer. Programming by strict definition requires proper training and practice time, commodities teachers find in short supply. However, by learning some commands the teacher might be able to develop some small and simple application programs to meet a particular learning situation. There are other programming languages such as Logo, Pascal, and additional languages such as PILOT. Each computer language serves a definite purpose. However, they are not considered as well-rounded in application and/or ease of use as BASIC. The creators of BASIC must have known what they were doing when they intended the B to stand for "beginners." Those who want to continue with their BASIC experiences as well as with other programming languages will find many good texts available.

Before You Begin

The BASIC commands that follow are written in short, concise, and easy-to-follow formats with self-explanatory features. This approach has proven successful for those teachers and students starting with computers for the first time.

First, an objective to be learned is presented. This is followed with a BASIC command for how the objective is to be achieved, as well as with the function of that command. Short and varied programs each with a title and comment section are then used to demonstrate the objective. Follow-up exercises are also presented to test what has been just learned. It is recommended that you keep in contact with a person who does know BASIC just in case you run into that seemingly unanswerable question.

And speaking of problems, you'll most likely encounter a few when you try to get your little programs to run correctly. If the computer gives you an error message for the program line you just entered, you can re-enter it by typing the line over again. You should also refer to your own computer's BASIC manual for guiding you through your errors (a list of programming errors is found in these manuals) as well as ways to edit or correct your program lines.

It is important that you follow the order of commands presented here since a spiral approach to learning is taken. The expression "practice makes perfect" is especially true when working with today's computers which by design do not have the foresight and flexibility in thinking that humans have. So don't expect miracles immediately, since your beginning experiences will be marked by the common expression: GIGO (Garbage In, Garbage Out).

Operating on Different Micros

First, find out how to turn on your own computer (sometimes a very trying task!) and access the BASIC language. The BASIC commands that follow are general enough to meet the specifications of the most commonly used micros in the schools today. However, there are some exceptions as indicated with the commands and keys listed in Table I. Please consult your operating manuals for any other minor discrepancies not listed in the table. For example, some micros will use semicolons, commas, and colons differently than described here, while others will require full typing of the commands as in the case where the command is IF-THEN instead of just IF.

The BASIC that follows was written using a TRS-80 model I, III, and IV. Refer to the TRS-80 listing in Table I and then find its equivalent command or key for your own micro.

Example:

```
10 CLS

20 PRINT "HI"          (TRS-80)

30 GOTO 10
```

is equivalent to

```
10 HOME

20 PRINT "HI"          (APPLE)

30 GOTO 10
```

Go to it!

Table I
Equivalent BASIC Commands and Keys for Microcomputers

Function / Type Micro	Storing lines in memory	Clearing screen	Exponentiation
TRS-80 I, III and IV	ENTER key	CLS	↑ key (I and III) CLEAR and (;) keys (IV)
APPLE II, II+, IIE	RETURN key	HOME	< key
COMMODORE 64/VIC 20	RETURN key	PRINT CHR$(147)	↑ key
ATARI	RETURN key	PRINT CHR$(125)	< key
IBM PC	RETURN key	CLS	< key
TI 99/4A	ENTER key	CALL CLEAR	< key

Function / Type Micro	Breaking program	Selecting random numbers	By way of INPUT
TRS-80 I, III, and IV	BREAK key	T = RND(10) (random integer from 1 to 10)	INPUT "YOUR NAME IS";N$ PRINT N$

Computer	Break/Stop	Random	Input/Print
APPLE II, II+, IIE	CTRL and C or CTRL and RESET keys	T = INT(10*RND (1)) + 1 (INT returns largest integer that is less than or equal to decimal number in parentheses)	INPUT "YOUR NAME IS";N$ PRINT N$
COMMODORE 64/ VIC 20	STOP or RESTORE and STOP keys	T = INT(10*RND (0) + 1)	INPUT "YOUR NAME IS";N$ PRINT N$
ATARI	BREAK key	T = INT(RND(0)*10) + 1	DIM N$ (20) PRINT "YOUR NAME IS" INPUT N$ PRINT N$ (must reserve space with DIM for string variables only)
IBM PC	CTRL and BREAK keys	RANDOMIZE T = INT(10*RND + 1) (RANDOMIZE is usually in beginning of program)	INPUT "YOUR NAME IS";N$ PRINT N$
TI 99/4A	CLEAR (FCTN 4) key	RANDOMIZE T = INT(10*RND) + 1 (RANDOMIZE is usually in beginning of program)	INPUT "YOUR NAME IS":N$ PRINT N$ (note use of colon after quotes; multiple commands with (:) on same line will not work with regular TI BASIC.)

```
RUN
COUNTING
HERE'S 1
NOW 2
THERE'S 3
LET'S DO IT
READY
>_
```

OBJECTIVE: Displaying information on your cathode ray tube (CRT).

HOW: PRINT statement.

FUNCTION: The PRINT statement will output on your screen (CRT) numbers, letters, and most any other character.

The "TYPE-IN" Section　　　　　*The "COMMENTS" Section*

A DEMONSTRATION

```
10 PRINT "COUNTING"
```
Pressing the (ENTER) key "enters" each program line into the computer's memory.

```
20 PRINT "HERE'S" 1
```

```
30 PRINT "NOW" 2
```
Number characters don't need quotes. Letter characters and just about everything else do require quotes.

```
40 PRINT "THERE'S" 3
```

```
50 PRINT "LET'S DO
   IT"
```
Don't forget to type number 0, *not* letter O, for line numbers.

```
RUN
```
Type RUN to run your program.

```
NEW
```
Don't forget to type NEW.

```
10 PRINT "S/HE"

20 PRINT "LOVES"

30 PRINT "ME"
```
After you RUN this program, do it again using semicolons and commas.

```
RUN
```

```
LIST
10 PRINT"S/HE";
20 PRINT"LOVES",
30 PRINT"ME"
READY
>RUN
S/HELOVES          ME
READY
>
```

```
NEW
```
Notice your output now! Semicolons and commas do special things when not in quotes. Can you explain? See below.

```
10 PRINT "S/HE";
```

```
20 PRINT "LOVES",
```
Semicolons join output together while commas space them a certain distance apart.

```
30 PRINT "ME"
```

```
RUN
```

LINE ORDERING

```
NEW

40 PRINT "RIGHT"

10 PRINT "THIS"

30 PRINT "THE"

20 PRINT "IS"

70 PRINT "NOW"

60 PRINT

50 PRINT "ORDER"

LIST

RUN
```

It might seem strange to you but type in this program as you see it. Don't forget to (ENTER) each line.

The PRINT in 60 outputs a blank line.

Type LIST to list the contents of the computer's memory and the actual order of execution.

FANCY STUFF

```
NEW

10 PRINT "HEY YOU!",
   "YEAH----> YOU"

20 PRINT "WHO"

30 PRINT "ME?"

RUN
```

What effect on your display does that comma have in line 10? Explain.

Our "arrow" in 10 is made with the "-" and ">" keys.

SPACING

```
NEW

10 PRINT "HI DAD AND
   MOM"

20 PRINT " LOOK AT
   ME"
```

The spaces in lines 20, 30, 40 and 50 are intentional.

Use the space bar to move LOOK over in 20. Do the same for the rest of the lines.

```
30 PRINT "  I'M ON"
```
Notice the slant of your output.
It was meant to look this way.

```
40 PRINT "   MY"
```

```
50 PRINT "    OWN"
```

```
RUN
```

Test Line Time

```
10 PRINT "THIS IS
   LINE" 10
```
Notice in 40 that numbers
should be in quotes if we use
non-numeric characters with
them such as the OR.

```
20 PRINT "AND THIS
   IS LINE" 20
```

```
30 PRINT "WHAT LINE
   IS THIS?"
```
If you attempt to input an answer to 40 the computer will not
respond since it is not pro-
grammed to do so. We will show
you how to input later.

```
40 PRINT "10,20, 30
   OR 40?"
```

Exercise Time!

1. Circle the letter of the program on the right which produces the
   output on the left. If you are not sure test each program out on
   your computer.

```
UP
DOWN
ABOVE
BELOW
```

```
A. 10 PRINT "UP"
      "DOWN" "ABOVE"
      "BELOW"
B. 10 PRINT "UP",
      "DOWN"
   20 PRINT "ABOVE",
      "BELOW"
C. 10 PRINT "UP"
   20 PRINT "DOWN"
   30 PRINT "ABOVE"
   40 PRINT "BELOW"
D. 10 PRINT "UP,
      DOWN, ABOVE,
      BELOW"
```

2. Use only one PRINT statement to achieve this type of output on the CRT:

```
FAR            FARTHER            FARTHEST
```

3. Use three PRINT statements to get this output:

```
TRY            TRY
TO             TO
REMEMBER       FORGET
```

4. Use PRINT statements to output in the middle of your screen a rocket ship like the one below;

```
                 X


        X            X


        X            X


        X            X
            XXX

            XXX
```

5. Determine what output the following program will give you:

```
10 PRINT "LAST NAME, FIRST NAME";
```

(TEST YOUR GUESS ON THE COMPUTER!)

6. Enter and run this program as you see it.

```
01 PRINT "ALPHABET TIME"

02 PRINT "A"

03 PRINT "B"

04 PRINT "D"

05 PRINT "E"

06 PRINT "F"
```

Using the above program, create a line for the letter C so that it is outputted between B and D. Do you see the importance of making line numbers at certain intervals such as 5, 10, 15, 20 . . . *or* 10, 20, 30 . . . *or* 3,6,9, 12 . . . *or* 1,3,5,7, ..??

7. Which non-numeric character cannot contain quotes? GUESS AND TEST!!!

```
10 PRINT ","

20 PRINT "."

30 PRINT """

40 PRINT "?"

50 PRINT "$"

60 PRINT "#"
```

Can you figure out why?

> OBJECTIVE: Changing the order of execution!
>
> HOW: GOTO statement.
>
> FUNCTION: The GOTO is an unconditional transfer statement which is used to change the normal sequence of executing your program.

The "TYPE-IN" Section   The "COMMENTS" Section

AN EXAMPLE

```
NEW
```
Line 10 is executed by the computer first.

```
10 PRINT "I'M AT
   LINE 10 NOW"
```
Then the GOTO 10 in line 20 instructs the computer to do line 10 again. This looping is done repeatedly. So we have
```
20 GOTO 10
```
10-20-10-20 . . .

```
RUN
```
Press (BREAK) to stop program.

```
LIST
10 PRINT" MIKE";
20 GOTO 10
READY
>RUN
 MIKE MIKE MIKE MIKE MIKE MIKE MIKE MIKE MIKE MIKE MIKE MIKE MIK
E MIKE MIKE MIKE MIKE MIKE MIKE MIKE MIKE MIKE MIKE MIKE MIKE MI
KE MIKE MIKE MIKE MIKE MIKE MIKE MIKE MIKE MIKE MIKE MIKE MIKE M
IKE MIKE MIKE MIKE MIKE MIKE MIKE MIKE MIKE MIKE MIKE MIKE MIKE
MIKE MIKE MIKE MIKE MIKE MIKE MIKE MIKE MIKE MIKE MIKE MIKE MIKE
 MIKE MIKE MIKE MIKE MIKE MIKE MIKE MIKE MIKE MIKE MIKE MIKE MIK
E
Break in 20
READY
>_
```

```
LIST
10 PRINT" JOSIE",
20 GOTO 10
READY
>RUN
 JOSIE          JOSIE          JOSIE          JOSIE
 JOSIE          JOSIE          JOSIE          JOSIE
 JOSIE          JOSIE          JOSIE          JOSIE
 JOSIE          JOSIE          JOSIE          JOSIE
 JOSIE          JOSIE          JOSIE          JOSIE
 JOSIE          JOSIE          JOSIE          JOSIE
 JOSIE          JOSIE          JOSIE          JOSIE
 JOSIE          JOSIE          JOSIE
Break in 10
READY
>_
```

Name in Lights

```
NEW

10 PRINT "          ";

20 GOTO 10
```

Type your name in between the quotes in line 10—leave 1 space between the first quote and your first name.

```
RUN

NEW

10 PRINT "       ",

20 GOTO 10

RUN
```

If you get nothing on the screen you didn't read the above.

Now do the program again. This time insert a comma at the end of 10. Note the difference between the 2 programs.

BORING STUFF

```
NEW

10 CLS

20 PRINT "I LIKE ME"

30 PRINT

40 PRINT "I AM GREAT
   BUT SLIGHTLY"

50 PRINT"REPETITIOUS"

60 GOTO 20

RUN
```

The CLS statement in 10 clears the screen before executing the next lines.

At line 60 the computer is instructed to start over at the top beginning with line 20. So we have this looping: 20-30-40-50-60-20-30-40-50-60 . . . until you stop it with the BREAK key.

STUCK ON 70

```
05 CLS

10 PRINT "HI MY NAME
   IS CLYDE
   COMPUTER"

20 PRINT

30 PRINT "I HAVE A
   PROBLEM"
```

Don't forget NEW before you enter this program.

The screen is not showing our usual cursor because 70 has a GOTO 70 which says go back to 70. So we have a 70-70-70 . . . sequence until you press the BREAK key.

```
40 PRINT "I AM STUCK
   AT LINE 70"

50 PRINT "AND CAN'T
   MOVE"

60 PRINT "WHY PICK
   ON ME?"

70 GOTO 70
```

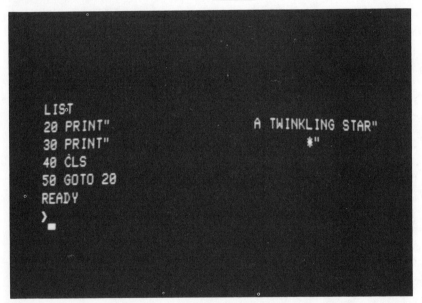

STAR TIME

```
20 PRINT " A
   TWINKLING STAR"

30 PRINT"          *       "

40 CLS

50 GOTO 20
```

Note that line 40 clears the screen and line 50 says go back to 20 and put it and everything to follow back on. This looping is done over and over. The sequence is 20-30-40-50-20-30-40-50. . .

The on and off effect of 20-30-40-50 . . . produces a blinking star!

GETTING DIZZY?

```
10 PRINT "HERE I AM
   AT 10"

20 GOTO 50

30 PRINT "AND NOW AT
   30"

40 GO TO 10

50 PRINT "CAUGHT ME
   AT 50"

60 GOTO 30
```

The line sequencing of this program is 10-20-50-60-30-
40-10-20-50-60-30-40-...

Note what is happening!

RUN the program several times
and note the different lines the
computer stops on when you
break the program.

TRY THESE!

1. Use the GOTO, CLS and PRINT statements to make your own
    name twinkle.

2. Explain what this program is doing.

```
10 PRINT "FREEZE - THIS IS A STICK-UP
20 GOTO 20
```

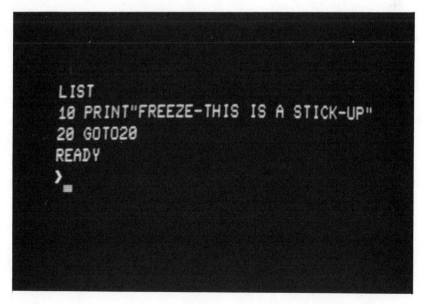

3.   Read the program and use a GOTO statement in line 40 to provide for the conclusion.

```
10 PRINT "KISS ME
   ONCE"

20 GOTO 50

30 PRINT "KISS ME
   NO"

40

50 PRINT "KISS ME
   TWICE"

60 GOTO 30

70 PRINT "MORE"
```

4.   Add a line that will make the question marks blink.

```
10 CLS

20 PRINT "  ?    ?  "

30 PRINT "  ? ? ?  "

40 CLS
```

5.   What program below will produce a continuous column of 5's until you break it?

```
A.  10 PRINT 5

    20 CLS

    30 PRINT 5
```

```
B.  10 PRINT 5;

    20 CLS

    30 GOTO 20

C.  10 PRINT 5

    20 GOTO 10

    30 CLS
```

OBJECTIVE: Working with calculations and numeric variables.

HOW: Numeric variables (represented by A, B, C, . . .
Z), LET (assignment) statements and arithmetic
functions.

FUNCTION: The computer can perform calculations with the
use of the PRINT statement and the values
stored in numeric variables.

FIVE ARITHMETIC FUNCTIONS

KEYBOARD CHARACTERS	FUNCTION
+ means ----------------	Addition
− means ----------------	Subtraction
★ means ----------------	Multiplication
/ means ----------------	Division
∧ means ----------------	Exponentiation (taking a number to a power).

```
LIST
10 PRINT"15 + 3=" 15+3
20 PRINT"15 - 3=" 15-3
30 PRINT"15 TIMES 3=" 15*3
40 PRINT"15 DIVIDED BY 3="15/3
READY
>RUN
15 + 3= 18
15 - 3= 12
15 TIMES 3= 45
15 DIVIDED BY 3= 5
READY
>
```

The "TYPE-IN" Section   *The "COMMENTS" Section*

A Demonstration without Variables

```
10 PRINT "15 + 3 ="
   15 + 3
```

The numbers and operations in quotes explain the actual results that will be outputted on the right.

```
20 PRINT "15 - 3 ="
   15 - 3
```

```
30 PRINT "15 TIMES
   3 =" 15 * 3
```

```
40 PRINT "15 DIVIDED
   BY 3 =" 15/3
```

A Demonstration with Numeric Variables

```
05 PRINT "A = 15 AND
   B = 3"
```

In line 10 the value 15 is assigned to the numeric variable A and stored in a distinct memory location of the computer.

```
10 LET A = 15
```

```
20 LET B = 3

25 PRINT "A + B = "A
   + B

30 PRINT "A - B = "A
   - B

35 PRINT "A TIMES B
   = "A * B

40 PRINT "A DIVIDED
   BY B = "A/B
```

B is being assigned the value 3 in line 20 and stored in another memory location.

The LET in front of the variables in 10 and 20 is optional.

Lines 25, 30, 35 and 40 will output the results of adding, subtracting, multiplying and dividing the values of A and B.

A numeric variable can be a combination of leading letters and numbers such as AB, IAM4, D2R2, C, YOU, etc.

EXPOUNDING ON EXPONENTS

```
LIST
10 PRINT "THE SQUARE OF 2 IS "2^2
20 PRINT "THE CUBE OF 2 IS "2^3
30 PRINT "THE FOURTH POWER OF 2 IS "2^4
Ready
RUN
THE SQUARE OF 2 IS  4
THE CUBE OF 2 IS  8
THE FOURTH POWER OF 2 IS  16
Ready
```

```
10 PRINT "THE SQUARE
   OF 2 IS " 2^2

20 PRINT "THE CUBE
   OF 2 IS " 2^3

30 PRINT "THE FOURTH
   POWER OF 2 IS "
   2^4
```

The exponentiation key will be represented on the TRS-80 IV as (∧). You need to press the (CLEAR) and (;) keys to get this.

Which Comes First?

```
10 A = 2

20 B = 4

30 C = 6

40 D = 1

50 PRINT A * B - C/A
   + D - B^2
```

In 50, as we go from left to right, exponentiation is always done first then multiplication or division is done next.

Addition or subtraction is done last.

Do the calculations by hand to check the answers! Are you convinced of the computer's accuracy?

A Fancy Formula

```
05 PRINT "WHAT'S THE
   DISTANCE?"

10 RATE = 10

20 TIME = 2

30 PRINT "DISTANCE =
   "RATE * TIME
   "MILES"
```

Numeric variables may be more than two characters but only the first two characters are usually read by the computer.

The numeric variables RATE and TIME are not in quotes in line 30.

Mixing It Up

```
10 MAD = 20

20 BAD = 40

30 PRINT BAD/20,
   MAD/40, SAD, BAD/
   MAD, MAD/BAD
```

The numeric variable SAD in 30 outputs a value of 0 since we never assigned it a number value.

Now Your Turn

1. Write a short program to produce exactly this output. The program should include use of arithmetic functions and numeric variables.

```
5 Times 5 = 25
5 Divided By 5 = 1
5 Minus 5 = 0
```

2. Use only one PRINT statement and some arithmetic functions that will produce this output after you type RUN.

```
RUN

5           10          15
```

3. Here's a mess of numbers! Get the computer to figure the final calculation any way you like.

   $23.59 - 8 + 42 \times 6 \div 12 - 7 \times 8.2^2$

4. Which program on the left will produce the exact output on the right?

```
A.  10 A = 4
    20 B = 6
    30 C = 7
    PRINT "A TIMES B TIMES C = "A × B × C

B.  PRINT "4 TIMES 6 TIMES 7 = "               168

C.  PRINT 4 * 6 * 7
```

TEST YOUR CHOICE!

5. Assign numeric values to the variables SUE and BOB so that Sue is five times as old as Bob and the sum of their ages is 18.

```
10  SUE =
20  BOB =
30  PRINT "THE SUM OF SUE'S AND BOB'S AGE IS"
    BOB + SUE
```

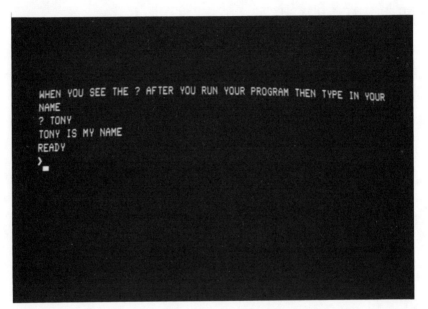

```
WHEN YOU SEE THE ? AFTER YOU RUN YOUR PROGRAM THEN TYPE IN YOUR
NAME
? TONY
TONY IS MY NAME
READY
>
```

OBJECTIVE: Interacting with your micro by way of input!

HOW: INPUT statement, string and numeric variables.

FUNCTION: The INPUT statement allows you to interact with the computer by entering numeric characters by means of a numeric variable and any other type of characters by means of a string variable.

The "TYPE-IN" Section   *The "COMMENTS" Section*

INPUTTING YOUR NAME

```
05  CLS
```

Line 20 contains a string variable: N$ (don't forget to include the $ after N). String variables

```
10 PRINT "WHEN YOU
   SEE THE ? AFTER
   YOU RUN YOUR
   PROGRAM THEN TYPE
   IN YOUR NAME"
```

can accept values which are alphabetic and numeric.

The computer will wait patiently in line 20 showing a question until you do something—like type your name!

```
20 INPUT N$
```

In 20 your name then becomes the value of N$ and it is outputted in line 30 by PRINT N$. N$ is not in quotes.

```
30 PRINT N$" IS MY
   NAME"
```

The value of N$ will change as you input different name values.

INPUTTING YOUR NUMBER

```
05 CLS

10 PRINT "WHEN YOU
   SEE THE ? AFTER
   YOU RUN YOUR
   PROGRAM THEN TYPE
   YOUR FAVORITE
   NUMBER"
```

Line 20 contains a numeric variable: N. It can only accept as input numeric values.

The value of N is outputted in line 30 by PRINT N.

```
20 INPUT N

30 PRINT N" IS MY
   FAVORITE NUMBER"
```

A VARIATION ON YOUR NAME

```
05 CLS

10 REM VARIATION OF
   INPUT

20 INPUT "WHEN YOU
   SEE THE? AFTER
   YOU RUN YOUR
   PROGRAM THEN TYPE
   YOUR NAME"; T$
```

Line 10 contains something new: REM. REM stands for remark. It is a nonexecutable statement which is usually used to tell you what your program line(s) is about.

```
TYPE IN YOUR NAME, THEN YOUR AGE? JAMES
?? 13
MY CURRENT NAME IS JAMES AND I'M  13 YEARS OLD
READY
>_
```

```
30 PRINT "MY NAME IS
   "T$
```

Lines 10 and 20 of the above programs can be combined into one line 20 here.

Two at a Time

```
05 CLS

10 REM ANOTHER WAY
   OF INPUTTING

20 INPUT "TYPE IN
   YOUR NAME, THEN
   YOUR AGE"; V$, A

30 PRINT "MY CURRENT
   NAME IS " V$" AND
   I'M "A" YEARS
   OLD"
```

After you RUN the program line 20 allows you to enter two things: your name and your age. After you type in your name press (ENTER) and then type your age and (ENTER) it.

The current value of V$ and A will be outputted in 30. Remember there are no quotes around V$ and A.

A Product Test

```
05 CLS

10 INPUT "TYPE IN
   ANY TWO NUMBERS
   AND I WILL
   MULTIPLY THEM";
   N, T
```

In line 20 the multiplication of the two values of the numeric variables N and T take place at the end: N*T.

```
TYPE IN ANY TWO NUMBERS AND I WILL MULTIPLY THEM? 5
?? 87
THE PRODUCT OF  5  AND  87  IS  435
CHECK IT IF YOU DON'T BELIEVE ME
READY
>_
```

```
20 PRINT "THE
   PRODUCT OF "N"
   AND "T" IS "N*T

30 PRINT "CHECK IT
   IF YOU DON'T
   BELIEVE ME"
```

Now Your Turn

1. Use the INPUT statement to output the name and age of your
    best friend. Don't forget to include string and numeric variables.

2. RUN the following program if enough information is given. If
    not enough information is given, include what is needed and then
    RUN it.

```
05 REM GOAL:  TO ADD TWO NUMBERS WITH AN
   INPUT STATEMENT
10 INPUT "TYPE IN TWO NUMBERS AND I WILL ADD
   THEM";
15 PRINT "THE SUM OF YOUR NUMBERS IS "A + B
```

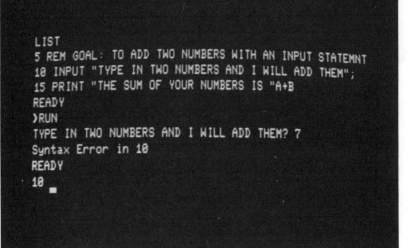

```
LIST
5 REM GOAL: TO ADD TWO NUMBERS WITH AN INPUT STATEMNT
10 INPUT "TYPE IN TWO NUMBERS AND I WILL ADD THEM";
15 PRINT "THE SUM OF YOUR NUMBERS IS "A+B
READY
>RUN
TYPE IN TWO NUMBERS AND I WILL ADD THEM? 7
Syntax Error in 10
READY
10 ■
```

3. Choose the program that will correctly output the name of your favorite TV program and the TV station it is on after your input.

```
A.  05 CLS
    10 PRINT "I LIKE "N$" ON STATION NUMBER
       "T
    15 INPUT N$, T


B.  05 CLS
    10 INPUT "MY FAVORITE SHOW IS"; V$
    20 INPUT "IT IS ON STATION"; L


C.  05 CLS
    10 PRINT "WHAT IS YOUR FAVORITE TV
       PROGRAM AND ITS STATION?"
    15 INPUT L$, V
    20 PRINT L$, V
```

4. Use the INPUT and PRINT statements to produce the following output (area of a triangle = ½ times the base times the height):

```
The base is         .
The height is          .
The area of your triangle is
```

5. Rewrite the *PRODUCT TEST* program. This time show the quotient of any two numbers you input and then show the difference of these same numbers.

OBJECTIVE: Making decisions.

HOW: IF-THEN statement.

FUNCTION: The IF-THEN statement tests a given condition. When the IF condition is true, the THEN part is executed. When the IF condition is not true, execution passes on to the next statement in the program.

The IF-THEN statement is usually used with these BASIC symbols on the right:

Meaning	Symbol
Greater Than	>
Less Than	<
Equal	=
Greater Than or Equal to	>=
Less Than or Equal To	<=
Not Equal	<>

SUMMARY: In the IF-THEN statement, when the *IF* part is true the *THEN* part is executed. When the *IF* part is false, the next line is executed.

The "TYPE-IN" Section	The "COMMENTS" Section

HERE'S AN EXAMPLE!

Here's the logic of this program:

```
05 INPUT "HOW OLD
ARE YOU"; V
```

1) Input your age

```
10 IF V<20 THEN
   PRINT "STILL
   YOUNG AND
   SWINGING": END

15 PRINT "BETTER
   TAKE IT SLOW:
   YOU'RE GETTING
   ANCIENT"
```

2) If age less than 20 then print "still . . ."and end program

3) If age is 20 or more then print "better . . ."and end program

The colon in 10 allows more commands per line. It is outside the quotes.

```
LIST
5 INPUT" HOW OLD ARE YOU ";V
10 IF V< 20 THEN PRINT "STILL YOUNG AND SWINGING":END
15 PRINT "BETTER TAKE IT SLOW: YOU'RE GETTING ANCIENT"
READY
>RUN
 HOW OLD ARE YOU ? 40
BETTER TAKE IT SLOW: YOU'RE GETTING ANCIENT
READY
>RUN
 HOW OLD ARE YOU ? 17
STILL YOUNG AND SWINGING
READY
>
```

NUMBER GUESS

The logic of this program is:

```
05 REM FINDING THE
   LOWER NUMBER

10 INPUT "GIVE ME
   ANY TWO NUMBERS
   AND I WILL GUESS
   THE LOWER ONE";
   A, B
```

1) Input any two numbers

2) If numbers are equal go back to beginning

3) If value of A is less than B then print A lower number and end program

```
20 IF A = B THEN
   PRINT "THEY ARE
   EQUAL": GOTO 10

30 IF A<B THEN PRINT
   "YOUR LOWER
   NUMBER IS "A: END

40 PRINT "YOUR LOWER
   NUMBER IS "B

50 END
```

4) Print B lower number and end program

CRAZINESS!

```
05 INPUT "TYPE YOUR
   NAME"; S$

10 PRINT "LET'S TRY
   YOUR LUCK "S$

15 INPUT "TYPE 'YES'
   OR 'NO'"; T$

20 IF T$ < > "NO"
   GOTO 10

30 PRINT "THANK
   GOODNESS THIS
   CRAZINESS IS
   OVER!"
```

The "<>" in 20 means not equal. If your input value from 15 is not equal to "NO" then you go back to 10.

JOKE TIME!

```
01 REM PICK ONE

05 L$ = "A PLANE!"

10 T$ = "SUPERFLY"

15 N$ = "A GARBAGE
   TRUCK"
```

If you answered the riddle "correctly" the first time but were told to do it again you probably didn't enter the value of N$ exactly as shown including spaces. Don't include quotes!

```
25 INPUT "WHAT HAS 4
   WHEELS AND
   FLIES"; M$

30 IF N$ = M$ THEN
   PRINT "YOU'RE
   RIGHT    "N$: END

35 PRINT "NOPE! TRY
   AGAIN"

40 GOTO 25
```

In line 30 your value of M$ is being compared with an already defined value of N$ from 15.

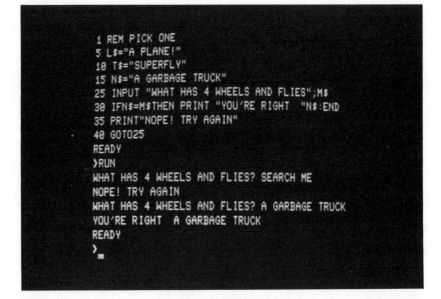

Now Your Turn

1. Read the following program, decide what it is suppose to be doing and then complete the IF part of the IF-THEN statement.

```
05 REM GUESSING LETTERS

10 INPUT "PICK YOUR FAVORITE LETTER"; N$

15 IF        THEN PRINT "YOUR LETTER IS "N$"
   AND IT IS AFTER M": END
```

```
20 PRINT "YOUR LETTER IS "N$" AND IT IS
   BEFORE N"
```

2. Change the *NUMBER GUESS* program so that the higher number is always outputted. Write your program here and then run it!

3. Determine what this program is doing and then test your guess on the micro!

```
10 C = 8

20 INPUT "2,4,6---WHAT NUMBER DO WE
   APPRECIATE"; R

30 IF C < > R THEN 60

40 PRINT "OBVIOUS RESPONSE - TRY AGAIN"

50 GOTO 20

60 PRINT "RIGHT - ANYTHING BUT EIGHT"

70 END
```

4. Create your own *JOKE TIME* program. Make up four possible responses to the old time favorite: WHAT IS BLACK, WHITE AND RED ALL OVER? Write your program below.

OBJECTIVE: Time to count.

HOW: Counting assignment statements.

FUNCTION: A counting assignment statement can be used for keeping a count of the current value of a variable.

The "TYPE-IN" Section   *The "COMMENTS" Section*

1, 2, 3, 4, 5 . . .

```
05 REM INCREASING BY
   ONES

10 PRINT "INCREASING
   G BY 1 IN G = G +
   1 "

20 G = 0
```

Line 25 contains a counting assignment statement: G = G + 1.

The G on the left of the "=" will always be 1 more than the G on the right of "=".

```
LIST
5 REM INCREASING BY ONES
10 PRINT "INCREASING G BY 1 IN G=G+1"
20 G=0
25 G=G+1
30 PRINT
40 PRINT"THE CURRENT VALUE OF G IS" G
50 GOTO25
READY
>
```

```
THE CURRENT VALUE OF G IS 32

THE CURRENT VALUE OF G IS 33

THE CURRENT VALUE OF G IS 34

THE CURRENT VALUE OF G IS 35

THE CURRENT VALUE OF G IS 36

THE CURRENT VALUE OF G IS 37

Break in 30
READY
>
```

```
25 G = G + 1

30 PRINT

40 PRINT "THE
   CURRENT VALUE OF
   G IS "G

50 GOTO 25
```

Here's how the loop works:

$$G = G + 1$$
$$1 \leftarrow 0 + 1$$
$$2 \leftarrow 1 + 1$$
$$3 \leftarrow 2 + 1$$
$$4 \leftarrow 3 + 1$$
.　.　.
.　.　.
.　.　.

2, 4, 6, 8 . . .

```
05 CLS

10 REM COUNTING BY
   2'S TO 100

15 S = 0

20 S = S + 2

25 PRINT "THE VALUE
   OF S IS NOW "S

30 IF S = 100 THEN
   END

35 GOTO 20
```

The counter statement in 20 is increasing S by 2's.

The loop is:
$$S = S + 2$$
$$2 \leftarrow 0 + 2$$
$$4 \leftarrow 2 + 2$$
$$6 \leftarrow 4 + 2$$
$$8 \leftarrow 6 + 2$$
$$\cdot \quad \cdot \quad \cdot$$
$$\cdot \quad \cdot \quad \cdot$$
$$\cdot \quad \cdot \quad \cdot$$

ODD – ISN'T IT?

```
05 REM ODDS TO 99

10 J = 1

20 PRINT "THE VALUE
   OF J IS NOW "J

30 J = J + 2

40 IF J = 101 THEN
   END

50 GOTO 20
```

The counter in 30 is acting this way in its loop:
$$J = J + 2$$
$$3 \leftarrow 1 + 2$$
$$5 \leftarrow 3 + 2$$
$$7 \leftarrow 5 + 2$$
$$9 \leftarrow 7 + 2$$
$$\cdot \quad \cdot \quad \cdot$$
$$\cdot \quad \cdot \quad \cdot$$
$$\cdot \quad \cdot \quad \cdot$$

101 is never outputted. Why?

10 NAMES

```
10 REM PRINT YOUR
   NAME 10 TIMES

20 C = 0
```

When $C = 10$ in line 60 the program ends.

```
LIST
10 REM PRINT YOUR NAME 10 TIMES
20 C=0
30 INPUT "YOUR NAME PLEASE";T$
40 PRINT"MY NAME IS "T$
45 C=C+1
50 PRINT"THE VALUE OF C IS "C
60 IF C=10 THEN END
70 GOTO 40
READY
>RUN
YOUR NAME PLEASE? TOMMY
```

```
MY NAME IS TOMMY
THE VALUE OF C IS   4
MY NAME IS TOMMY
THE VALUE OF C IS   5
MY NAME IS TOMMY
THE VALUE OF C IS   6
MY NAME IS TOMMY
THE VALUE OF C IS   7
MY NAME IS TOMMY
THE VALUE OF C IS   8
MY NAME IS TOMMY
THE VALUE OF C IS   9
MY NAME IS TOMMY
THE VALUE OF C IS  10
READY
>
```

```
30 INPUT "YOUR NAME
   PLEASE"; T$

40 PRINT "MY NAME IS
   "T$

45 C = C + 1
```

```
50 PRINT "THE VALUE
   OF C IS "C

60 IF C = 10 THEN
   END

70 GOTO 40
```

You Do These

1. Alter the *1, 2, 3, 4, 5* . . . program so that it stops counting at 100. You need only add one line.

2. Choose from the right side the correct output of the program on the left:

```
10 T = 5                    A.  5, 10, 15...100
15 PRINT T;
20 T = T + 5                B.  5
30 IF T = 100 THEN
   END                      C.  10, 15, 20...40
35 GOTO 20
                            D.  NOTHING
```

3. Write and run a program following this flow of thinking:

<pre>
            INPUT YOUR
            LAST NUMBER
                 ↓
       ┌→ COUNTER =
       │ COUNTER + 1
       │   WRITE   PRINT
       │   COUNTER   LAST
   NO └── IS LAST NUMBER = YES EQUALS → NUMBER
           COUNTER?   LAST   AND
                      →   NUMBER   END
</pre>

4. Suppose you received a nickel a day for exactly one month (30 days). Write and run a program using a counting assignment statement to determine the sum of money for each day of the month.

OBJECTIVE: Performing repeated tasks the easy way

HOW: FOR-NEXT loop.

FUNCTION: The FOR-NEXT loop allows you to do tasks repeatedly without the need of IF-THEN and
counting statements.

FORMAT:

FOR X =   J   TO   H
  ↑   ↑   ↑

(Counter   (Starting   (Ending
variable-   number goes   number goes
keeps track here)   here)
of count)

... TASKS TO BE REPEATED ...
... GO HERE INSIDE LOOP ...

NEXT X

↑
(Calls next
  number in loop)

The "TYPE-IN" Section   *The "COMMENTS" Section*

HERE GOES!

```
05 REM READY FOR A
   FOR-NEXT DEMO?

10 FOR Y = 1 TO 5

20 PRINT "MY NAME IS
   COMPUTER"

30 NEXT Y
```

The contents of line 20 will be
outputted 5 times. It is inside
the FOR (line 10) and NEXT
(line 30) loop which counts
from 1 to 5.

```
LIST
5 REM READY FOR A FOR-NEXT DEMO?
10 FOR Y=1 TO 5
20 PRINT "MY NAME IS COMPUTER"
30 NEXT Y
READY
>RUN
MY NAME IS COMPUTER
MY NAME IS COMPUTER
MY NAME IS COMPUTER
MY NAME IS COMPUTER
MY NAME IS COMPUTER
READY
>
```

1 to 10

```
05 REM COUNTING TO
   10 BY ONES
```

Actually anything can be inside a FOR-NEXT loop.

```
10 FOR G = 1 TO 10
```

Here we are outputting the numbers from 1 to 10 (line 20).

```
20 PRINT G
```

```
30 NEXT G
```

JUMPING AHEAD

```
05 REM COUNTING BY
   THREES
```

The STEP 3 in line 10 increases each number by 3 starting with 0.

```
10 FOR S = 0 TO 100
   STEP 3
```

The last number outputted will be 99 since we can't go past 100.

```
20 PRINT S
```

```
30 NEXT S
```

```
LIST
10 INPUT"TYPE IN ANY WHOLE NUMBER"; N
20 FOR Y=1 TO N
30 PRINT"GOING" Y
40 IFN=Y THEN PRINT"GONE AT "N:END
50 NEXT Y
READY
>RUN
TYPE IN ANY WHOLE NUMBER? 4
GOING 1
GOING 2
GOING 3
GOING 4
GONE AT  4
READY
>_
```

WHEN TO STOP

```
10 INPUT "TYPE IN
   ANY WHOLE
   NUMBER"; N
```

In 10 we input a whole number that will serve as our end number in the loop.

```
20 FOR Y = 1 TO N

30 PRINT "GOING "Y

40 IN N = Y THEN
   PRINT "GONE AT
   "N: END
```

In 40 our input number N is being compared with our counting number Y. When Y equals N, the program will end.

```
50 NEXT Y
```

BACKWARDS NOW

```
10 PRINT "COUNT
   DOWN"

20 FOR L = 100 TO 1
   STEP - 1

30 PRINT L
```

In line 30 the STEP - 1 allows us to count backwards from 100 to 1 by 1's.

```
40 NEXT L

50 PRINT "BLAST OFF"
```

SLOWING IT DOWN

```
10 REM SLOW MOTION

20 FOR X = 1 TO 50

30 PRINT "THIS IS
   EXCITING"

40 FOR Y = 1 TO
   1000: NEXT Y

50 NEXT X
```

Line 40 contains a FOR-NEXT loop with nothing inside. With this type of loop the computer counts to itself from 1 to 1000. It is normally used to slow down your output.

ON YOUR OWN TIME

1. What will be the correct output on the right using the program on the left?

```
10 FOR X = 1 TO 3        A.  X
20 PRINT X                   X
30 NEXT X                    X

                         B.  X X X

                         C.  1
                             2
                             3

                         D.  1 2 3
```

2. Change the *JUMPING AHEAD* program to output multiples of 5; that is: 0, 5, 10, 15 . . .

3. Fix up this program so that it will count backwards from 150. What line(s) is causing the problem?

```
10 REM BACKWARDS
20 FOR X = 1 TO 150
   STEP - 1
30 PRINT X
40 NEXT X
```

4. What's wrong with this program?

```
10 REM WRONG?
20 FOR G = 1 TO 10
30 PRINT X
40 NEXT G
```

5. Use an INPUT statement to change the *SLOWING IT DOWN* program to any speed you desire.

Chapter 7

MORE BASIC COMMANDS

OBJECTIVE: Randomizing.

HOW: RND function.

FUNCTION: The *RND* function generates random numbers
               which are often used in simulations such as edu-
               cational games.

The "TYPE-IN" Section   *The "COMMENTS" Section*

AN EXAMPLE

```
05 REM FIRST TRY

10 T = RND(10)

20 PRINT T
```

In line 10 RND (10) selects only
one random number from 1 to
10 and stores it in T. RUN program 5 times and keep a record
of each random number.

END TIME

```
05 REM GOING FOR THE
   END
```

In 15 the RND function is
choosing a random number
from 1 to 25.

157

```
15 F = RND(25)

18 PRINT F

20 IF F = 25 THEN
   PRINT "THIS IS
   THE END": END

25 PRINT "TRY
   AGAIN!"

27 FOR X = 1 TO
   1000: NEXT X

30 GO TO 15
```

In 20 if the random number happens to be 25 the program ends.

GUESS A NUMBER

```
05 REM GUESS MY
   NUMBER 1-10

15 N = RND(10)

20 INPUT "PICK A
   NUMBER FROM 1 TO
   10"; T

30 IF T<N THEN INPUT
   "TOO LOW-TRY
   AGAIN"; T:   GO TO
   30

40 IF T>N THEN INPUT
   "TOO HIGH-GO
   AGAIN"; T:   GO TO
   30

50 IF T=N PRINT "YOU
   GOT IT-WHAT A
   GUESSER!"

60 END
```

Study the comparisons (<, >, =) being made in lines 30, 40, 50 respectively.

Do you think you understand what's happening? Are you sure?

```
LIST
5 REM GUESS MY NUMBER 1-10
15 N=RND(10)
20 INPUT "PICK A NUMBER FROM 1 TO 10";T
30 IF T<N THEN INPUT"TOO LOW-TRY AGAIN";T:GOTO 30
40 IF T>N THEN INPUT "TOO HIGH-GO AGAIN";T:GOTO 30
50 IF T=N PRINT "YOU GOT IT-WHAT A GUESSER!"
60 END
READY
>RUN
PICK A NUMBER FROM 1 TO 10? 5
TOO HIGH-GO AGAIN? 3
TOO HIGH-GO AGAIN? 2
YOU GOT IT-WHAT A GUESSER!
READY
>_
```

Random Count

```
10 REM COUNT TO END

20 X = RND(1023)

30 FOR G = 1 to X

40 PRINT G

50 NEXT G

60 INPUT "GO AGAIN
   (TYPE Y OR N)";
   T$

70 IF T$="Y" THEN 20

80 CLS

90 PRINT "THAT'S IT
   FOLKS"
```

The random value of X in line 20 becomes the end number in the loop of line 30.

```
ROLL   1 IS  4 AND  5
ROLL   2 IS  2 AND  2
ROLL   3 IS  4 AND  4
ROLL   4 IS  6 AND  6
ROLL   5 IS  4 AND  5
ROLL   6 IS  6 AND  5
ROLL   7 IS  4 AND  2
ROLL   8 IS  4 AND  3
ROLL   9 IS  1 AND  5
ROLL  10 IS  2 AND  2
ROLL  11 IS  1 AND  5
ROLL  12 IS  2 AND  5
THIS IS YOUR LUCKY DAY
READY
>_
```

```
ROLL  1 IS  2 AND  6
ROLL  2 IS  4 AND  2
ROLL  3 IS  5 AND  6
ROLL  4 IS  1 AND  1
WHOOPS---SNAKE-EYES YOU LOSE!!
READY
>_
```

Dice Roll

```
01 REM ROLLING
   AGAINST SNAKE-
   EYES 12 CHANCES
   TO WIN

05 CLS
```

Line 50 has a logical connector AND. Others are OR and NOT.

```
10 D1 = RND(6)

20 D2 = RND(6)

30 C = C + 1

40 PRINT "ROLL "C"
   IS "D1" AND "D2

50 IF D1 = 1 AND D2
   = 1 PRINT "WHOOPS
   -- SNAKE-EYES YOU
   LOSE!!": END

60 IF C = 12 THEN
   PRINT "THIS IS
   YOUR LUCKY DAY":
   END

70 GOTO 10
```

How would you slow this program down?

You Do These

1. Which program below will output one random number from 1 to 100?

```
A.  10 PRINT RND(100)
    20 GOTO 10
```

```
C.  10 K = RND(100)
    20 PRINT K
    30 GOTO 10
```

```
B.  10 REM THIS IS IT
    20 L = RND(100)
    30 PRINT L
```

2. Add commands to 10 and 20 below so that you will have the computer randomly pick and multiply any two numbers from 1 to 50.

```
10

20

30 PRINT "THE PRODUCT OF "N" AND "T" IS "N *
   T
```

3.   Add a counter to *GUESS A NUMBER* that will tell you how many tries it took you to guess the number. Experiment by changing the random number to a number higher than 10.

4.   Run the following program a few times (say 5). What could be a problem with it and why?

```
10 REM RANDOM BEGIN AND END
20 Y = RND(50)
30 X = RND(20)
40 FOR T = X TO Y
50 PRINT T
60 NEXT T
```

5.   Change the *DICE ROLL* program to roll 12 times. If you get 6 on each die you lose!

OBJECTIVE: Reading data.

HOW: READ and DATA statements.

```
LIST
5 REM READING A NUMBER
10 READ A
20 PRINT A
30 DATA 10
READY
>RUN
 10
READY
>
```

FUNCTION: The *READ* and *DATA* statements are used together to allow for the reading of numeric and
non-numeric information.

The "TYPE-IN" Section   *The "COMMENTS" Section*

TAKING A LOOK

```
05 REM READING A
   NUMBER

10 READ A

20 PRINT A

30 DATA 10
```

A is a number variable referring
to number 10 in line 30.

The READ and DATA state-
ments go together. One will not
operate without the other.

A NON-NUMBER

```
10 READ B$

20 PRINT B$

30 DATA MY NAME IS
   HUGO
```

B$ is a non-numeric variable re-
ferring to MY NAME IS
HUGO in line 30.

NAMES AND NUMBERS

```
10 READ C$, D

20 PRINT C$, D

30 DATA MY NUMBER IS
   , 22
```

The comma is necessary in line
10. It separates each piece of
data being read in line 30.

TOO MUCH DATA

```
10 READ S

20 PRINT S

30 DATA 10, 20, 30,
   40, 50, 60
```

Notice that just the number 10
has been outputted. The program will only READ one piece
of data (the first one) unless you
tell it otherwise with something
like the next program.

A DIFFERENT WAY

```
10 FOR X = 1 TO 6
```
Since we are reading 6 numbers, we can use a FOR-NEXT loop and set our end number to 6.

```
20 READ S

30 PRINT S

40 NEXT X

50 DATA 10, 20, 30,
   40, 50, 60
```

ANOTHER WAY

```
10 READ G
```
Line 40 tells the computer to READ another piece of data. However, we will get an OD error (out of data) when we RUN this program. This means the computer is looking for more data after the 7 in line 30.

```
20 PRINT G

30 DATA 30, 40, 55,
   7

40 GOTO 10
```

```
LIST
10 READ G
20 PRINT G
30 DATA 30,40,55,7
40 GOTO 10
READY
)RUN
 30
 40
 55
 7
Out of DATA in 10
READY
)
```

```
LIST
10 READ G
15 IF G=999 THEN END
20 PRINT G
30 DATA 30,40,55,7,999
40 GOTO 10
READY
>RUN
 30
 40
 55
 7
READY
>
```

15 IF G = 999 THEN
   END

We can fix this program with a "flag" and IF-THEN statement. Change line 30 and add line 15.

Now run the program.

30 DATA 30,40,55,7,
   999

The flag number is "999". It could be any number which signals an end to READ before it prints out the "999".

You Do These

1. Use a READ and DATA statement to output the name of your best friend and his/her age.

2. Choose from the right side the correct output of the program on the left.

```
10 PRINT "HI"                    A. HI
20 READ A, B, C
30 DATA 10, 20, 30               B. HI
                                    10, 20, 30

                                 C. 10, 20, 30

                                 D. NOTHING
```

```
LIST
10 FORX=1 TO 10
20 READ A
30 PRINT A;
40 DATA 3,6,5
50 DATA 7,8,9
60 DATA 12,14,1,2
READY
>RUN
 3
READY
>
```

GUESS AND TEST

3. Predict the output of the following program before you RUN it.

```
10 FOR X = 1 TO 10

20 READ A

30 PRINT A;

40 DATA 3, 6, 5

50 DATA 7, 8, 9

60 DATA 12, 14, 1, 2
```

4. Modify *ANOTHER WAY* so that it READS and outputs 6 of your favorite pet animals. Don't forget to use a "flag" to end your READ-DATA statements.

5. What program on the right will produce the exact output on the
    left?

```
A.  10  READ A$,B$,C$
    20  PRINT A$,B$,C$
    30  DATA ZERO,
        ZERO, ZERO
```

0

0

0

```
B.  10  READ A
    20  PRINT A
    30  DATA 0, 0, 0
```

```
C.  10  READ A, B, C
    20  PRINT A, B, C
    30  DATA 0, 0, 0
D.  NONE
```

OBJECTIVE: Adding it up.

HOW: Assignment statements.

FUNCTION: Working with numeric quantities such as adding
a grocery bill or a list of numbers is done in a certain way with assignment statements.

The "TYPE-IN" Section   *The "COMMENTS" Section*

AN ADDING NUMBERS DEMO

```
10  REM ADDING 5
    NUMBERS

20  T = 0

30  CLS

40  INPUT "GIVE ME A
    NUMBER"; N

50  T = T + N
```

In line 50 the value of T on the
left is changed by the value of T
on the right and the number
you enter, N. We initialize T =
0 in line 20.

```
>LIST
10 REM ADDING 5 NUMBERS
20 T=0
30 CLS
40 INPUT" GIVE ME A NUMBER";N
50 T=T+N
60 C=C+1
70 IFC=5 THEN GOTO100
80 PRINT"YOUR TOTAL SO FAR IS"T
90 PRINT " GO AGAIN":GOTO 40
100 PRINT" THAT'S ADDITION!- YOUR FINAL SUM IS" T
READY
>
```

```
 GIVE ME A NUMBER? 9
YOUR TOTAL SO FAR IS 9
 GO AGAIN
 GIVE ME A NUMBER? 4
YOUR TOTAL SO FAR IS 13
 GO AGAIN
 GIVE ME A NUMBER? 2
YOUR TOTAL SO FAR IS 15
 GO AGAIN
 GIVE ME A NUMBER? 8
YOUR TOTAL SO FAR IS 23
 GO AGAIN
 GIVE ME A NUMBER? 7
 THAT'S ADDITION!- YOUR FINAL SUM IS 30
READY
>
```

```
60 C = C + 1

70 IF C = 5 THEN
   GOTO 100

80 PRINT "YOUR TOTAL
   SO FAR IS "T
```

If you entered the numbers 1,2 and 3 this is how line 50 adds them:

$$T = T + N$$
$$1 \leftarrow 0 + 1$$
$$3 \leftarrow 1 + 2$$
$$6 \leftarrow 3 + 3$$

```
90 PRINT "GO AGAIN":
   GOTO 40

100 PRINT "THAT'S
    ADDITION! - YOUR
    FINAL SUM IS "T
```

SHOPPING TIME

```
05 CLS

10 REM WHAT'S MY
   BILL?

15 G = 0

20 FOR X = 1 TO 3

30 READ A$, O

40 PRINT A$,   O

50 G = G + O

60 DATA MILK, 1.89

70 DATA STEAK, 2.56

80 DATA ALFALFA,
   4.09

90 NEXT X

100 PRINT

110 PRINT "TOTAL =
    "G
```

In line 30 the variable O is the letter not the number.

$$G = \quad G + \quad O$$
$$1.89 \leftarrow \quad 0 + 1.89$$
$$4.45 \leftarrow 1.89 + 2.56$$
$$8.54 \leftarrow 4.45 + 4.09$$

ADDING ANY AMOUNT

```
05 CLS
```

Line 20 allows us to control the end number of our FOR-NEXT loop in 30.

```
10 REM ADDING
   COUNTING NUMBERS
   TO WHATEVER??

15 R = 0

20 INPUT "STARTING
   WITH 1 HOW HIGH
   DO YOU WANT TO
   GO"; K

30 FOR X = 1 TO K

35 PRINT "THE SUM OF
   "R" AND "X" IS"

40 R = R + X

45 PRINT R

50 NEXT X

60 PRINT "AND THE
   FINAL SUM OF THE
   FIRST "K"
   COUNTING NUMBERS
   IS (A DRUM ROLL
   --- PLEASE!!)...
   ....." R
```

In line 35 the first value of R = 0 and X = 1. The R on the left represents the sum of the values of R and X on the right in line 40.

$$R = R + X$$
$$1 \leftarrow 0 + 1$$
$$3 \leftarrow 1 + 2$$
$$6 \leftarrow 3 + 3$$
$$10 \leftarrow 6 + 4$$
$$. \quad . \quad .$$
$$. \quad . \quad .$$
$$. \quad . \quad .$$

Now You Go

1. Change *AN ADDING NUMBERS DEMO* to find the product of the first five counting numbers. Line 50 must have a multiplication formula and for 20 initialize T = 1. Why?

2. Predict the outcome of the following program. Then test your guess by running it.

```
10 CLS

20 INPUT "TYPE ANY NUMBER"; N
```

```
LIST
10 CLS
20 INPUT"TYPE ANY NUMBER";N
30 J=J+N
40 IFJ)=1000 THEN PRINT "YOU'VE REACHED THE LIMIT":END
50 GOTO20
READY
>RUN
```

```
30 J = J + N

40 IF J> = 1000 THEN PRINT "YOU'VE REACHED
   THE LIMIT": END

50 GOTO 20
```

3. Choose the program on the right which produces the output on
    the left.

```
A.  10 FOR T = 1 TO 3
    20 X = X + T
    25 PRINT X
    30 NEXT T


B.  10 FOR M = 1 to 3
    20 Y = Y + M
    30 PRINT N
    40 NEXT M


C.  10 FOR J = 1 TO 3
    20 L = L + J
    30 NEXT J
    40 PRINT L
```

6

```
LIST
10 CLS
20 REM CREATING A NUMBER LIST CALLED T
30 DIM T(13)
40 FORX=1 TO 13
50 INPUT "ANY NUMBER PLEASE";T(X)
60 PRINT T(X)" IS IN ROW "X
70 NEXT X
80 PRINT "THIS IS WHAT YOUR LIST CONTAINS"
90 FORX= 1 TO 13
100 PRINT T(X)" IS IN ROW "X
110 NEXT X
READY
>
```

```
THIS IS WHAT YOUR LIST CONTAINS
 6  IS IN ROW  1
 7  IS IN ROW  2
 2  IS IN ROW  3
 90 IS IN ROW  4
 45 IS IN ROW  5
 23 IS IN ROW  6
 8  IS IN ROW  7
 34 IS IN ROW  8
 21 IS IN ROW  9
 5  IS IN ROW  10
 20 IS IN ROW  11
 9  IS IN ROW  12
 87 IS IN ROW  13
READY
>
```

OBJECTIVE: Storing your data.

HOW: DIM statement.

FUNCTION: Allows us to reserve in the computer's memory
             spaces for storing data as a list or array.

The "TYPE-IN" Section	*The "COMMENTS" Section*

FIRST TIME

```10 CLS```	In line 30 we must first dimension (DIM) a list that is, give a name to the list (here T) and tell how many rows in T (here 13).

```20 REM CREATING A```
 ```   NUMBER LIST```
 ``` CALLED T```	

```30 DIM T(13)```	T(X) in 50 is used to receive and store our 13 numbers.
```40 FOR X = 1 TO 13```	
```50 INPUT "ANY NUMBER``` ``` PLEASE"; T(X)```	
```60 PRINT T(X)" IS IN``` ``` ROW "X```	
```70 NEXT X```	

```80 PRINT "THIS IS```
 ```   WHAT YOUR LIST```
 ``` CONTAINS"```	

```90 FOR X = 1 TO 13```	
```100 PRINT T(X)" IS``` ``` IN ROW "X```	
```110 NEXT X```	

RANDOM LIST

```05 CLS```	Line 35 assigns a random number from 1 to 100 to a slot in array L.

```10 REM 20 RANDOM```
 ```   ASSIGNMENTS TO```
 ``` LIST L```	

```15 DIM L(20)```	
```30 FOR Y = 1 TO 20```	

```
35 X = RND (100)

40 L(Y) = X

45 PRINT "HERE'S
   WHAT IT LOOKS
   LIKE!"

50 PRINT "ROW "Y"
   HAS "L(Y) "IN IT"

60 INPUT "DO IT
   AGAIN - YES OR NO
   ";L$

65 IF L$ = "YES"
   THEN 70

68 PRINT "END": END

70 NEXT Y

80 PRINT "YOU
   REACHED ROW "Y
   "TIME TO QUIT!"
```

LIST L(20)

1._____
2._____
3._____
  .
  .
  .
20._____

An option to quit the program before reaching row 20 is given in line 60.

ADDING TWO ARRAYS

```
05 CLS

10 REM ADDING ROWS
   IN TWO ARRAYS

20 DIM B(15), C(15)

25 FOR Y = 1 TO 15

30 X = RND(100):'
   B(Y) = X

35 Z = RND(100):
   C(Y) = Z
```

In lines 30 and 35 random numbers are being assigned to arrays B and C. Each array has 15 slots or rows.

B(15)	+	C(15)	
1.___	+	1.___	=
2.___	+	2.___	=
3.___	+	3.___	=
.		.	
.		.	
.		.	
15.___	+	15.___	=

```
50 PRINT "B"Y" IS
   "B(Y)" C" Y" IS
   "C(Y)" THEIR SUM
   IS "B(Y)+C(Y)
```

Line 50 will output the sum of each list. Be careful of the quotes.

```
60 INPUT "ANOTHER GO
   AT IT - YES OR
   NO"; T$
```

```
65 IF T$ = "YES"
   THEN 70
```

```
68 PRINT "NO - GO":
   END
```

```
70 NEXT Y
```

YOUR TURN NOW

1. Choose the correct output from the right for the program on the left.

A.   5
       10
       15
        .
        .
        .
      100

B.   0
        5
       10
        .
        .
        .
      200

```
10 DIM G(400)
20 FOR Y = 0 TO 200
   STEP 5
30 G(Y) = Y
40 PRINT G(Y)
50 NEXT Y
```

C.   0
        5
       10
        .
        .
        .
      400

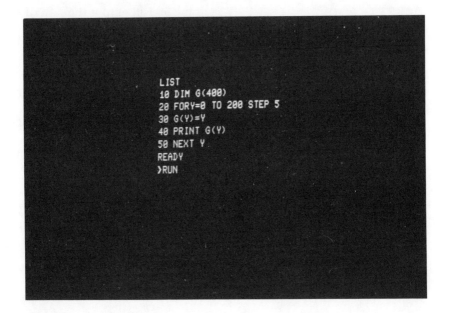

```
LIST
10 DIM G(400)
20 FORY=0 TO 200 STEP 5
30 G(Y)=Y
40 PRINT G(Y)
50 NEXT Y
READY
>RUN
```

2. Alter a *RANDOM LIST* so that only 50 random numbers are assigned to list L.

3. Figure out the error in the following program, fix it up, and run the program correctly.

```
10 DIM C(15), G(15)
15 FOR X= 1 TO 15
20 INPUT "PICK ANY TWO NUMBERS AND I WILL
   SAVE THEM AND SHOW YOU THE DIFFERENCE";
   T,S
30 C(Y) = T
40 G(Y) = S
50 PRINT "THEIR DIFFERENCE IS" C(Y)-G(Y)
60 NEXT X
```

OBJECTIVE: Using subroutines.

HOW: GOSUB and RETURN statements.

FUNCTION: The GOSUB in conjunction with RETURN allows the user to perform a certain task (or subroutine) within a program.

```
LIST
10 REM GOSUB-RETURN
20 CLS:INPUT "TYPE'D' FOR A DEMO";N$
30 IF N$<>"D" THEN 20
40 GOSUB 75
50 INPUT"TYPE 'A' IF YOU WANT TO DO IT AGAIN";E$
60 IFE$="A" THEN 40
70 CLS:PRINT"END":END
75 C=C+1
80 CLS:PRINT"YOU MADE IT NUMBER " C:PRINT
90 PRINT"CONGRATULATIONS"
100 RETURN
READY
>
```

FORMAT: GOSUB # (a line number somewhere in
             program)
             - - - - - -
             # - - (tasks to be performed)
             - - - - - -
             RETURN   (placed right after subroutine-
                       execution of program goes to line
                       after GOSUB statement)

The "TYPE-IN" Section   *The "COMMENTS" Section*

AN EXAMPLE

```
10 REM GOSUB -
   RETURN
```
Typing "D" initiates GOSUB at 40. Control goes immediately to the subroutine.

```
20 CLS: INPUT "TYPE
   'D' FOR A DEMO";
   N$
```
The subroutine consists of lines 75, 80, and 90.

```
30 IF N$ < > "D"
   THEN 20
```
After line 90 control returns to line 50—the line after the GOSUB.

```
RUN
TYPE'D' FOR A DEMO? D
YOU MADE IT NUMBER  1

CONGRATULATIONS
TYPE 'A' IF YOU WANT TO DO IT AGAIN? A
YOU MADE IT NUMBER  2

CONGRATULATIONS
TYPE 'A' IF YOU WANT TO DO IT AGAIN? A
YOU MADE IT NUMBER  3

CONGRATULATIONS
TYPE 'A' IF YOU WANT TO DO IT AGAIN?
```

```
40 GOSUB 75

50 INPUT "TYPE 'A'
   IF YOU WANT TO DO
   IT AGAIN"; E$

60 IF E$ = "A" THEN
   40

70 CLS: PRINT "END":
   END

75 C = C + 1

80 PRINT "YOU MADE
   IT NUMBER" C:
   PRINT

90 PRINT
   "CONGRATULATIONS"

100 RETURN
```

More than One

```
05 REM SEVERAL
   GOSUBS
```

Do you remember what line 20 does?

```
10 CLS: PRINT: PRINT
   "READY--SET--"

20 FOR X = 1 TO 1000
   : NEXT X


30 GOSUB 70

40 GOSUB 90

50 GOSUB 110

60 PRINT: PRINT
   "YOUR COMPUTER
   LOVES YOU ": END

70 PRINT "ROSES ARE
   RED"

75 FOR X = 1 TO
   1000: NEXT X

80 RETURN

90 PRINT "VIOLETS
   ARE BLUE"

95 FOR X = 1 TO
   1000: NEXT X

100 RETURN

110 PRINT "FEELING
    FINE BECAUSE
    ....."

115 FOR X = 1 TO
    1000: NEXT X

120 RETURN
```

Lines 30,40, and 50 call different subroutines.

The subroutines are at lines:
$$70 - 75$$
$$90 - 95$$
$$110 - 115$$

Line 60 is executed after the last RETURN in 120.

JACKPOT

```
10 REM PLAYTIME

20 N = RND(5)

30 CLS: PRINT "GUESS
   MY NUMBER-IT'S
   FROM 1 TO 5"

40 INPUT T

50 IF N=T GOSUB 100:
   END

60 IF N<>T GOSUB 140

70 INPUT "TYPE 'P'
   TO PLAY AGAIN";
   P$

80 IF P$ = "P" THEN
   20

90 PRINT "DON'T
   FORGET PLAYTIME":
   END

100 CLS: FOR X = 1
    TO 25

110 CLS: PRINT
    "*******************"

120 NEXT X: PRINT
    "YOU GOT IT"

130 RETURN

140 CLS: FOR X = 1
    TO 25

150 CLS:
    PRINT"?    ?    ?"
```

There are 2 subroutines in this program. Where are they?

Your chances of getting the correct number the first time are 20%—not very good!

```
160 NEXT X:
    PRINT"SORRY YOU
    MISSED IT"

170 RETURN
```

Your Turn Now

1. Study the following program. Find out why it doesn't run. The desired output should be HI THERE. Fix it up!

```
10 REM SOMETHING WRONG

20 GOSUB 40

30 GOSUB 50

40 PRINT "HI"

50 RETURN

60 PRINT "THERE"

70 RETURN
```

2. Predict the output of the following program, then test your guess.

```
10 REM WHAT IS IT?

20 INPUT "WHAT'S YOUR FIRST NAME"; F$

30 INPUT "WHAT'S YOUR MIDDLE NAME"; M$

40 INPUT "WHAT'S YOUR LAST NAME"; L$

50 GOSUB 90

60 GOSUB 100

70 GOSUB 110
```

```
75 PRINT "THAT'S IT FOLKS---THERE AIN'T NO
   MORE": END

80 PRINT

90 PRINT "LAST NAME - "L$: RETURN

95 RETURN

100 PRINT "FIRST NAME - "F$: RETURN

105 RETURN

110 PRINT "MIDDLE NAME - "M$: RETURN

115 RETURN
```

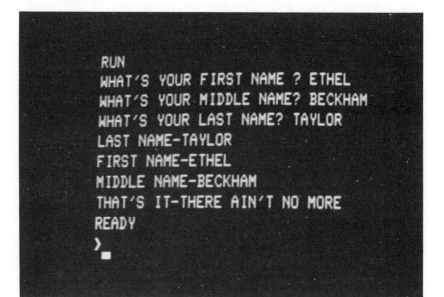

```
LIST
10 INPUT "PRESS 'G' TO GO";G$
20 IFG$<>"G" THEN 10
30 GOSUB 50
40 END
50 PRINT"I THERE
60 PRINT"GOOD
70 RETURN
80 PRINT"GOOD LOOKING"
READY
>RUN
PRESS 'G' TO GO? G
```

3. Choose the correct output on the right for the program on the left.

```
10 INPUT "PRESS 'G'          HI THERE
   TO GO"; G$

20 IF G$ <> "G"
   THEN 10

30 GOSUB 50                  HI THERE
                             GOOD

40 END

50 PRINT "HI THERE"

60 PRINT "GOOD"              HI THERE
                             GOOD LOOKING

70 RETURN

80 PRINT "GOOD
   LOOKING"
```

```
HOW MANY  SCORES DO YOU WANT TO AVERAGE? 4
TYPE IN SCORE  1
? 45
TYPE IN SCORE  2
? 90
TYPE IN SCORE  3
? 87
TYPE IN SCORE  4
? 34
```

Chapter 8

SOME BASIC APPLICATIONS
BY TEACHERS

RATIONALE

The following BASIC programs were devised by classroom teachers. Some of them are novel and humorous while others serve a purpose in the classroom. Each comes with its own documentation (see REM statements) so one can see how the variables and commands are put together to perform a simple task.

There is essentially nothing new presented that was not covered in the previous two chapters. In other words, given some time, some work, and a bit of imagination, teachers and students can put together commands to perform a task. And, of course, the value of the variables can be changed to meet one's needs.

The intent in presenting these programs is to stimulate the juices of some teachers and students in creating something from scratch. The rewards are personally satisfying and highly contagious.

AVERAGES

```
10 REM FINDING AN AVERAGE

20 REM--N REPRESENTS THE NUMBER OF SCORES
```

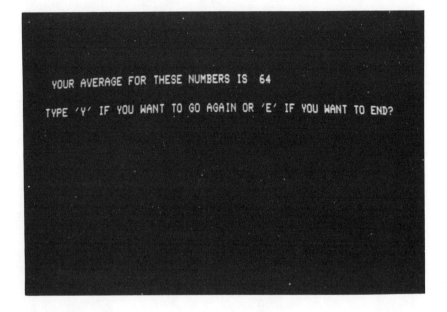

YOUR AVERAGE FOR THESE NUMBERS IS 64

TYPE 'Y' IF YOU WANT TO GO AGAIN OR 'E' IF YOU WANT TO END?

```
30   CLS:INPUT"HOW MANY SCORES DO YOU WANT TO
     AVERAGE";N

40 REM------- INITIALIZE TOTAL SUM S IN
   SUMMATION FORMULA

50   S=0

60 REM --LOOP BEGINS

70   FORX= 1 TO N

80     REM -----X KEEPS COUNT OF EACH SCORE

90       PRINT"TYPE IN SCORE "X

100      REM ----- A REPRESENTS THE VALUE OF
         EACH SCORE

110      INPUT A
```

```
120    REM-----THE SUMMATION FORMULA

130     S=S+A

140 NEXT X

150 REM--END LOOP

160 REM---TOTAL S DIVIDED BY NUMBER OF
    SCORES N

170  CLS:PRINT" YOUR AVERAGE FOR THESE
     NUMBERS IS "S/N

180 REM---------- CHOICE TO QUIT D$

190  PRINT:INPUT"TYPE 'Y' IF YOU WANT TO GO
     AGAIN OR 'E' IF YOU WANT TO END";D$

200  IF D$="Y"THEN 30

210 IF D$<>"Y"AND D$<>"E"THEN 190

220 CLS:PRINT"KEEP AVERAGING ---SEE YOU
    LATER"
```

Finding Perimeter

```
10 REM DISTANCE AROUND A SIMPLE CLOSED-SIDED
   FIGURE

20 REM----------- INITIALIZE VARIABLE P FOR
   PERIMETER

30 P=0

40 REM----------INPUT NUMBER OF SIDES H

50 CLS:INPUT" HOW MANY SIDES DOES YOUR
   FIGURE HAVE";H

60 REM----BEGIN LOOP
```

```
HOW MANY SIDES DOES YOUR FIGURE HAVE? 5
THE LENGTH OF SIDE  1  IS
? 7
 THE LENGTH OF SIDE  2  IS
? 4
  THE LENGTH OF SIDE  3  IS
? 8
 THE LENGTH OF SIDE  4  IS
? 3
  THE LENGTH OF SIDE  5  IS
? 6
```

```
70     FORX=1 TO H

80    REM---X KEEPS COUNT OF SIDES

90     PRINT" THE LENGTH OF SIDE "X" IS

100     REM---S IS THE LENGTH OF EACH SIDE

110      INPUT S

120     REM--------- THE SUMMATION FORMULA

130     P=P+S

140     NEXT X

150 REM--- END LOOP

160 REM----F$ REPRESENTS TYPE OF FIGURE

170 CLS:INPUT"NOW TELL ME WHAT TYPE OF
     FIGURE IS IT---FOR EXAMPLE A TRIANGLE,
     AN OCTAGON, AN I DON'T KNOW, ETC";F$
```

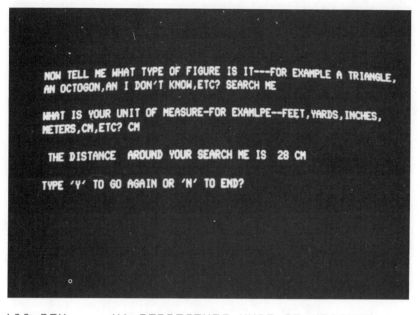

```
180  REM-----U$ REPRESENTS UNIT OF MEASURE

190  PRINT:INPUT"WHAT IS YOUR UNIT OF
     MEASURE-FOR EXAMPLE--FEET, YARDS,
     INCHES, METERS, CM, ETC";U$

200  REM---- YOUR RESULTS

210  PRINT:PRINT" THE DISTANCE AROUND YOUR
     "F$" IS " P;U$

220  REM------GO AGAIN

230  PRINT:INPUT"TYPE 'Y' TO GO AGAIN OR 'N'
     TO END";N$

240  IF N$ = "Y" THEN 20

250  REM-----------------

260  CLS:PRINT"I ENJOYED IT --- HURRY BACK
     SOON"
```

```
READY FOR A MULIPLICATION FACT TEST?????----HERE   GOES.........
.ASHLEY LESLEY KIMBERLEY
WHAT IS  5  TIMES  3 ??????
? 6

NO THAT'S NOT RIGHT- TRY AGAIN
WHAT IS  5  TIMES  3 ??????
? ■
```

MULTIPLICATION PRACTICE

```
10 REM MULTIPLICATION FACTS PRACTICE

20 REM--------NAME INPUT N$

30 CLS:INPUT" I WOULD LIKE TO KNOW YOUR
   FIRST NAME.IF YOU THINK I'M BEING A BIT
   TOO PERSONAL AND EVEN NOSY PLEASE TYPE IN
   ANYTHING YOU DESIRE";N$

40 CLS:PRINT"READY FOR A MULTIPLICATION FACT
   TEST?????----HERE     GOES......." N$

50 REM---------- FOR-NEXT TO SLOW THINGS
   DOWN

60 FOR C=1 TO 1000:NEXT C

70 REM--------N1,N2 STORE RANDOM FACTORS

72 REM-----C=# RIGHT; W=# WRONG
```

```
75 C=0:W=0

80 N1=RND(10)

90 N2=RND(10)

100 REM-------- MULTIPLICATION FORMULA

110 REM---------P=PRODUCT

120 P=N1*N2

130 PRINT" WHAT IS "N1 " TIMES " N2 "?????"

140 REM-------R IS USER INPUT

150 INPUT R

160 REM--------TEST USER INPUT R WITH
    PRODUCT P

165 REM----C=C+1 KEEPS TRACK OF NUMBER RIGHT

170 IF P=R THEN C=C+1:GOTO 200

172 REM----W=W+1 KEEPS TRACK OF NUMBER WRONG

175 W=W+1

180 PRINT :PRINT " NO THAT'S NOT RIGHT-TRY
    AGAIN":GOTO 130

190 REM ----- IF YOU ARE RIGHT

200 CLS:PRINT" GOOD JOB   "N$

210 REM----------DO IT AGAIN??????

220 PRINT " HOW ABOUT ANOTHER ?"

230 INPUT" TYPE 'M' FOR MORE OR 'N' FOR NO
    MORE AND RESULTS";M$
```

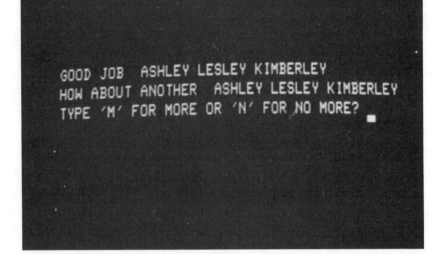

```
240 IF M$="M"THEN 80
260 PRINT:PRINT"YOUR SCORE WAS " C" RIGHT
    AND " W" WRONG

270 PRINT:PRINT"CATCH YOU LATER"
```

CELSIUS AND FAHRENHEIT

```
10 REM-----A LOOK AT CELSIUS TEMPERATURE

20 CLS:PRINT"HAVEN'T YOU NOTICED CELSIUS
   TEMPERATURE APPEARING MORE OFTEN WITH OUR
   CUSTOMARY FAHRENHEIT????????"

30 PRINT:PRINT"ISN'T IT ABOUT TIME YOU GOT
   SERIOUS AND LEARNED IT BEFORE THEY
   ELIMINATE FAHRENHEIT COMPLETELY???"

40 REM-------WANT TO LEARN CELSIUS?? (R$ IS
   RESPONSE)
```

```
50 INPUT"TYPE 'Y' FOR YEAH I WANT TO LEARN
   AND 'N' FOR NO THANKS I'VE DONE FINE UP
   TO NOW";R$

60 IF R$="N" THEN 520

70 REM------SOME CELSIUS MEANINGS

80 CLS:PRINT" I'M GLAD YOU MADE THAT CHOICE-
   HERE ARE SOME CELSIUS TEMPERATURES WITH
   INTERPRETATIONS"

90 REM----BEGIN LOOP ( 5 EXAMPLES )

100    FOR X=1 TO 5

110 REM---A$ AS DEGREES,B$ AS INTERPRETATION

120    READ A$,B$

130    PRINT

140    PRINT A$,B$

150 REM------THE DATA

160   DATA 100 DEGREES    ,WATER BOILS

170   DATA 37 DEGREES    ,NORMAL BODY
      TEMPERATURE

180   DATA 35 DEGREES   , A NICE HOT SUMMER
      DAY

190   DATA 22-26 DEGREES , COMFORTABLE ROOM
      TEMPERATURE

200   DATA 0 DEGREES    , WATER FREEZES

210   NEXT X
```

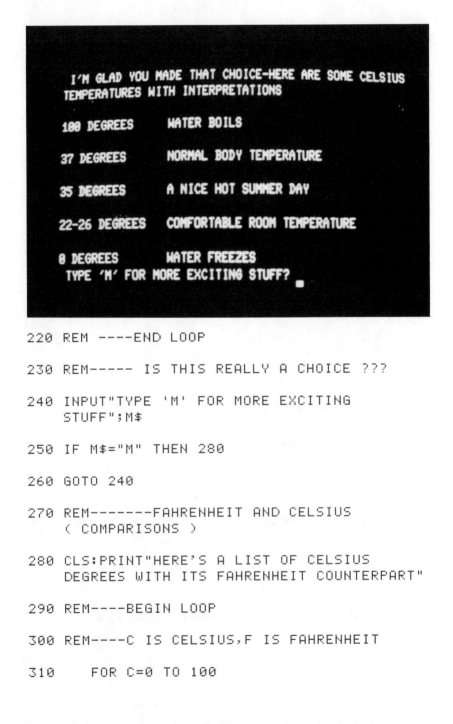

```
220 REM ----END LOOP

230 REM----- IS THIS REALLY A CHOICE ???

240 INPUT"TYPE 'M' FOR MORE EXCITING
    STUFF";M$

250 IF M$="M" THEN 280

260 GOTO 240

270 REM-------FAHRENHEIT AND CELSIUS
    ( COMPARISONS )

280 CLS:PRINT"HERE'S A LIST OF CELSIUS
    DEGREES WITH ITS FAHRENHEIT COUNTERPART"

290 REM----BEGIN LOOP

300 REM----C IS CELSIUS,F IS FAHRENHEIT

310   FOR C=0 TO 100
```

```
WHEN F IS    120.2 THEN C IS    49 DEGREES

WHEN F IS    122 THEN C IS    50 DEGREES
SOME HOT SPOT NEAR THE EQUATOR

WHEN F IS    123.8 THEN C IS    51 DEGREES

WHEN F IS    125.6 THEN C IS    52 DEGREES

WHEN F IS    127.4 THEN C IS    53 DEGREES
```

```
320    REM----- CELSIUS TO FAHRENHEIT
       CONVERSION FORMULA

330    F=1.8*C+32

340    PRINT:PRINT"WHEN F IS "F" THEN C IS
       "C" DEGREES"

350    REM------ SOME CELSIUS INTERPRETATIONS

360    REM----- FOR SPECIFIC VALUES OF C

370    IF C=100 THEN PRINT"WATER BOILS HERE"

380    IF C=0 THEN PRINT"WATER FREEZES AT
       THIS TEMP"

390    IF C=24 PRINT"THIS IS COMFORTABLE
       ROOM TEMP"

400    IF C=37 PRINT" YOUR NORMAL BODY TEMP"
```

```
DON'T FALL ASLEEP NOW THIS WILL GET EXCITING


WHEN F IS    60.8 THEN C IS    16 DEGREES


WHEN F IS    62.6 THEN C IS    17 DEGREES


WHEN F IS    64.4 THEN C IS    18 DEGREES


WHEN F IS    66.2 THEN C IS    19 DEGREES
```

```
410     IF C=35 THEN PRINT" THAT NICE HOT
        SUMMER DAY"

420     IF C=50 PRINT" SOME HOT SPOT NEAR THE
        EQUATOR"

430     IF C=15 THEN CLS:PRINT"DON'T FALL
        ASLEEP NOW THIS WILL GET EXCITING"

440     IF C=70 THEN PRINT"HUMAN DEHYDRATION
        TEMPERATURE"

450     IF C=85 PRINT"THAT CRACKED EGG ON THE
        SIDEWALK  IS NOW DONE"

460 REM---SLOWING IT DOWN

470      PRINT:FOR X=1 TO 500:NEXT X

480     NEXT C

490 REM---END LOOP

500 REM-------

510 PRINT"NICE BEING WITH YOU":END

520 CLS:PRINT"I'LL GET YOU ANOTHER TIME"
```

WE CAN ESTIMATE A CAR'S BRAKING DISTANCE.BRAKING DISTANCE IS
DEFINED AS THE DISTANCE TRAVELED BY A CAR AFTER THE DRIVER
APPLIES THE BRAKES AND WHEN THE AUTO STOPS COMPLETELY

IN ORDER TO FIND BRAKING DISTANCE WE NEED TO KNOW:
        1) THE CAR'S RATE OF SPEED
        2) THE TYPE AND CONDITION OF THE ROAD
PRESS 'F' IF YOU ARE FINISHED READING?

BRAKING DISTANCE

```
10 REM-------- HOW FAR AFTER BRAKING????

20 REM---------DEFINITION

30 CLS:PRINT"WE CAN ESTIMATE A CAR'S BRAKING
   DISTANCE. BRAKING DISTANCE IS DEFINED AS
   THE DISTANCE TRAVELLED BY A CAR AFTER THE
   DRIVER APPLIES THE BRAKES AND WHEN THE
   AUTO STOPS COMPLETELY

40 REM-----------------------------

50 PRINT:PRINT"IN ORDER TO FIND BRAKING
   DISTANCE WE NEED TO KNOW:

60 PRINT"        1) THE CAR'S RATE OF SPEED

70 PRINT"        2) THE TYPE AND CONDITION
   OF THE ROAD

80 INPUT"PRESS 'F' IF YOU ARE FINISHED
   READING";F$

90 IF F$<>"F" THEN 80
```

```
100 REM--------R EQUALS RATE OF SPEED

110 CLS:INPUT"FIRST TYPE IN THE RATE OF
    SPEED (MILES PER HOUR) YOU ARE GOING--
    FOR EXAMPLE: 25,67,55,100,ETC.";R

120 REM---------TYPES AND CONDITIONS OF
    ROADS

130 CLS:PRINT"NOW CHOOSE ONE NUMBER FROM THE
    MENU BELOW THAT BEST DESCRIBES THE TYPE
    AND CONDITION OF YOUR ROAD"

140 PRINT

150 PRINT" 1 ASPHALT AND DRY

160 PRINT" 2 ASPHALT AND WET

170 PRINT" 3 CONCRETE AND DRY

180 PRINT" 4 CONCRETE AND WET
```

```
NOW CHOOSE ONE NUMBER FROM THE MENU BELOW THAT BEST DESCRIBES
THE TYPE AND CONDITION OF YOUR ROAD

    1    ASPHALT AND DRY
    2    ASPHALT AND WET
    3    CONCRETE AND DRY
    4    CONCRETE AND WET
    5    GRAVEL AND DRY
    6    GRAVEL AND WET
    7    PACKED SNOW

NOW TYPE IN YOUR NUMBER? 3
```

```
190 PRINT" 5 GRAVEL AND DRY

200 PRINT" 6 GRAVEL AND WET

210 PRINT" 7 PACKED SNOW

220 REM--------N IS USER CHOICE

230 REM--------B$ IS TYPE AND SURFACE
    POSSIBILITIES

240 PRINT:INPUT" NOW TYPE IN YOUR NUMBER";N

250 IF N=1 THEN B$="ASPHALT AND DRY"

260 IF N=2 THEN B$="ASPHALT AND WET"

270 IF N=3 THEN B$="CONCRETE AND DRY"

280 IF N=4 THEN B$="CONCRETE AND WET"

290 IF N=5 THEN B$="GRAVEL AND DRY"

300 IF N=6 THEN B$="GRAVEL AND WET"

310 IF N=7 THEN B$="PACKED SNOW"

320 REM-------F IS TYPE-SURFACE ROAD
    CONSTANT

330 ON N GOTO 350 , 360 , 370 , 380 , 390 ,
    390 , 400

340 REM---IF N=1 THEN WE GO TO LINE 350; IF
    N=2 THEN LINE 360;ETC.

350 F=.85:GOTO430

360 F=.65:GOTO430

370 F=.90:GOTO430
```

```
380 F=.60:GOTO430

390F=.65:GOTO430

400 F=.45:GOTO430

410 REM--------THE BRAKING FORMULA

420 REM---------B=BRAKING DISTANCE

430 B=(R*R)/(30*F)
440 REM----- SLOWING OUTPUT DOWN

450 FOR X=1 TO 1000:NEXT X

460 REM------YOUR RESULTS

470 CLS:PRINT" TRAVELING AT " R "MILES PER
    HOUR AND ON "B$" ROADS   YOUR CAR WILL
    TAKE " B " FEET TO STOP COMPLETELY
```

TRAVELING AT 85 MILES PER HOUR AND ON CONCRETE AND DRY ROADS
YOUR CAR WILL TAKE 267.593 FEET TO STOP COMPLETELY

HOW ABOUT ANOTHER TRY-TYPE 'Y' FOR YES OR 'N' FOR NO?

```
480 REM------------------------

490 PRINT:INPUT" HOW ABOUT ANOTHER TRY-TYPE
    'Y' FOR YES OR 'N' FOR NO";I$

500 IF I$="Y"THEN 110

510 CLS:PRINT" SAFE DRIVING PLEASE--NOW THAT
    YOU ARE WISER"
```

Vowel Test

```
10 CLS

20 REM    VOWEL TEST --THE FIVE BASIC VOWELS

30 REM  IDEAS BY SAMBRA REDICK,ST JOHN'S HS,
   DARLINGTON, SC 29532

40 REM-------L$ STORES USER INPUT

50 INPUT"TYPE IN ANY LETTER AND I WILL TELL
   YOU IF IT IS A VOWEL";L$

60 REM-------RESETS READ COUNTER AT START OF
   DATA

70 RESTORE

80 REM-------BEGIN LOOP

90    FORV=1 TO 5

100    REM--T$ IS VALUE OF VOWEL

110     READ T$

120 REM--COMPARE USER INPUT L$
    TO T$

130    IF L$=T$ THEN 200
```

```
TYPE IN ANY LETTER AND I WILL TELL YOU IF IT IS A VOWEL? F
 YOUR INPUT  F IS  NOT A VOWEL
PRESS SPACE BAR AND THEN ENTER TO GO AGAIN OR ANY LETTER TO END?

TYPE IN ANY LETTER AND I WILL TELL YOU IF IT IS A VOWEL? A
 YOUR LETTER  A IS A VOWEL
PRESS SPACE BAR AND THEN ENTER TO GO AGAIN OR ANY LETTER TO END?
```

```
140 REM--WHEN T$ IS NOT EQUAL TO L$

150    NEXT V

160 REM--END LOOP

170  REM--OUTPUT WHEN T$ IS NOT EQUAL TO L$

180    PRINT " YOUR INPUT   " L$ " IS NOT A
         VOWEL":GOTO220

190  REM--OUTPUT WHEN T$ IS EQUAL TO L$

200  PRINT " YOUR LETTER " L$ " IS A VOWEL"

210 REM--E$ TO EXIT OR CONTINUE

220    INPUT"PRESS SPACE BAR AND THEN ENTER
         TO GO AGAIN OR ANY LETTER TO END";E$

230 REM--IF E$ IS EQUAL TO SPACE BAR---→ " "
```

```
240   IF E$=" "THEN 50

250 REM--IF E$ IS NOT

260   CLS:PRINT"SEE YOU LATER":END

270 REM------------------------------------

280   DATA A,E,I,O,U
```

CRICKET RANGE

```
10 REM GIVEN:HEAT AND A CRICKET

20 REM--------------------

30 CLS:PRINT "DID YOU KNOW THERE IS A
   RELATIONSHIP BETWEEN THE NUMBER OF TIMES
   A CRICKET CHIRPS IN ONE MINUTE AND
   CELSIUS (C) TEMPERATURE??
```

DID YOU KNOW THERE IS A RELATIONSHIP BETWEEN THE NUMBER OF TIMES A CRICKET CHIRPS IN ONE MINUTE AND CELSIUS (C) TEMPERATURE???

FOR EXAMPLE--IF THE TEMPERATURE OUTSIDE IS 26C (79F) THEN OUR FRIENDLY CRICKET WOULD CHIRP 154 TIMES IN ONE MINUTE

WHY DON'T YOU GIVE ME A TEMPERATURE IN CELSIUS (FROM 0 TO 100) AND I WILL INFORM YOU OF THE PER MINUTE CHIRPING ACTIVITY OF OUR FRIEND? 4

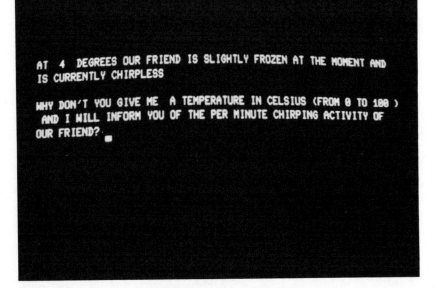

```
40 REM--------AN EXAMPLE

50 PRINT:PRINT"FOR EXAMPLE--IF THE
   TEMPERATURE OUTSIDE IS 26C (79F) THEN OUR
   FRIENDLY CRICKET WOULD CHIRP "7*(26-4) "
   TIMES IN ONE MINUTE

60 REM----------INPUT TEMPERATURE T

70 PRINT:INPUT"WHY DON'T YOU GIVE ME A
   TEMPERATURE IN CELSIUS (FROM 0 TO 100)
   AND I WILL INFORM YOU OF THE PER MINUTE
   CHIRPING ACTIVITY OF OUR FRIEND";T

80 REM----------- TEST TEMPERATURE
   BOUNDARIES:LINES 100-200

90 REM----------- WITH GOSUBS IN LINES 110,
   130,150
```

```
100 CLS:IF T>=0 AND T<=4 THEN PRINT"AT "T"
    DEGREES OUR FRIEND IS SLIGHTLY FROZEN AT
    THE MOMENT AND IS CURRENTLY CHIRPLESS
    ":GOTO70

110 REM--------------------

120  CLS:IF T>4 AND T<=15 THEN  PRINT" OUR
     CRICKET AT "T" DEGREES IS RECOVERING
     FROM THE EFFECTS OF A RECENT HARD
     FREEZE.WARMER DAYS ARE AHEAD.HANG IN
     THERE MR(S). CRICKET!!":
     GOSUB220  :GOTO 70

130 REM--------------------

140 CLS:IFT>15 AND T<=45 THEN PRINT" OUR
    FRIEND IS IN HIS GLORY WITH A TEMP OF
    "T" DEGREES.NICE HOT WEATHER IS
    HOPEFULLY HERE TO STAY.GO DO IT
    CRICKET!!!!":GOSUB 220  :GOTO70

150 REM--------------------

160 CLS:IFT>45 ANDT<=90 THEN PRINT " THINGS
    ARE GETTING KIND OF HECTIC FOR OUR
    FRIEND WITH A HIGH TEMP OF "T." THE
    PEOPLE ACROSS THE WAY ARE THINKING OF
    TAKING SERIOUS ACTION DUE TO THE
    EXCESSIVE NOISE":GOSUB 200  :GOTO70

170 REM-------------TOO MUCH HEAT

180 CLS:IF T>90 AND T<=100 PRINT" ACCORDING
    TO RECENT ACCOUNTS THE INTENSITY OF "
    7*(T-4) " CHIRPS PER MINUTE AT "T"
    DEGREES WAS SO GREAT THAT EVEN OUR
    LITTLE FRIEND COULDN'T HANDLE
    IT":PRINT"RIP":END
```

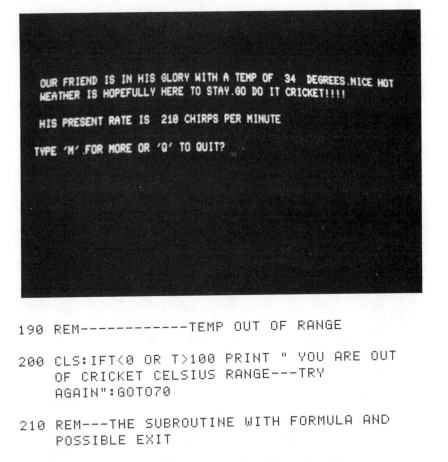

```
190 REM------------TEMP OUT OF RANGE

200 CLS:IFT<0 OR T>100 PRINT " YOU ARE OUT
    OF CRICKET CELSIUS RANGE---TRY
    AGAIN":GOTO70

210 REM---THE SUBROUTINE WITH FORMULA AND
    POSSIBLE EXIT

220 PRINT:PRINT" HIS PRESENT RATE IS
    "7*(T-4) " CHIRPS PER MINUTE

230 PRINT

240 INPUT"TYPE 'M' FOR MORE OR 'Q' TO
    QUIT";M$

250 PRINT

260 IF M$="Q" THEN PRINT" GOOD SHOW!!!":END

270 RETURN
```

A Spanish Quiz

```
10 REM SPANISH VOCAB TIME--IDEAS BY ALBERT
   WRIGHT,ST.JOHN'S HS,DARLINGTON, SC 29532

20 REM----N$ IS USER NAME

30 CLS:INPUT"TYPE IN YOUR FIRST NAME AND
   THEN WE'LL DO SOME SPANISH TOGETHER--
   SI?";N$

40 REM---BEGIN LOOP 10 WORDS

50 FOR X=1 TO 10

60 REM-------A$ STORES THE SPANISH

70  READ A$

80  DATA LA TIZA,THE CHALK,EL LIBRO, THE
    BOOK,LA PIZARRA,THE BLACKBOARD,EL
    ESTUDIANTE,THE STUDENT, LA CLASE,THE
    CLASS,EL CUADERNO, THE NOTEBOOK,LAS
    PREGUNTAS,THE QUESTIONS,EL PAPEL,THE
    PAPER, EL EXAMEN, THE TEST,EL PUPITRE,
    THE DESK

90 PRINT:PRINT" PLEASE TYPE THE CORRECT
   ENGLISH ( INCLUDING THE DEFINITE ARTICLE)
    FOR " A$

100 REM-----R$ IS USER RESPONSE

110 INPUT R$

120 REM--------THIS A$ STORES THE ENGLISH
    TRANSLATION

130 REM--------WHICH IS AFTER THE SPANISH IN
    DATA STATEMENT

140 READ A$
```

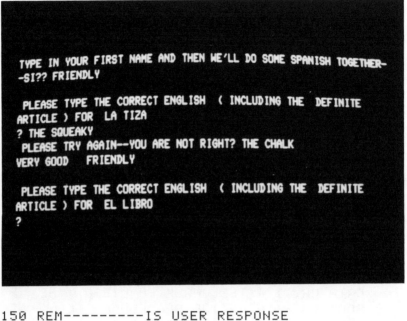

```
TYPE IN YOUR FIRST NAME AND THEN WE'LL DO SOME SPANISH TOGETHER-
-SI?? FRIENDLY

 PLEASE TYPE THE CORRECT ENGLISH ( INCLUDING THE  DEFINITE
ARTICLE ) FOR  LA TIZA
? THE SQUEAKY
 PLEASE TRY AGAIN--YOU ARE NOT RIGHT? THE CHALK
VERY GOOD    FRIENDLY

 PLEASE TYPE THE CORRECT ENGLISH ( INCLUDING THE  DEFINITE
ARTICLE ) FOR  EL LIBRO
?
```

```
150 REM---------IS USER RESPONSE
    CORRECT?????

160 IF R$=A$ THEN PRINT "VERY
    GOOD   "N$:GOTO 210

170 REM-----USER INCORRECT

180 INPUT"PLEASE TRY AGAIN--YOU ARE NOT
    RIGHT";R$: GOTO 160

190 REM-------THANKS FOR YOUR TIME

200 REM-------SIGNAL TO END WHEN 10TH WORD
    READ

210 IF X=10 THEN CLS:PRINT"GRACIAS PARA SU
    TIEMPO"

220 NEXT X

230 REM---END LOOP
```

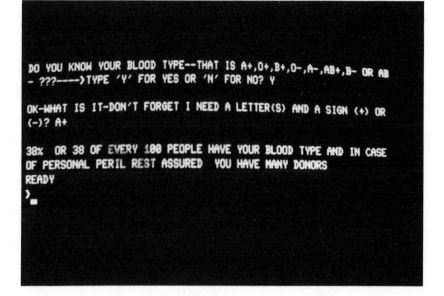

DO YOU KNOW YOUR BLOOD TYPE--THAT IS A+,O+,B+,O-,A-,AB+,B- OR AB
- ???---->TYPE 'Y' FOR YES OR 'N' FOR NO? Y

OK-WHAT IS IT-DON'T FORGET I NEED A LETTER(S) AND A SIGN (+) OR
(-)? A+

38% OR 38 OF EVERY 100 PEOPLE HAVE YOUR BLOOD TYPE AND IN CASE
OF PERSONAL PERIL REST ASSURED YOU HAVE MANY DONORS
READY
>

BLOOD TYPES

```
10 REM WHERE DOES YOUR BLOOD BELONG????

20 REM-------THE BLOOD TYPES

30 CLS:INPUT"DO YOU KNOW YOUR BLOOD TYPE--
   THAT IS A+,O+,B+,O-,A-,AB+,B- OR AB- ???
   ---- TYPE 'Y' FOR YES OR 'N' FOR NO";N$

40 IF N$<>"Y" AND N$<>"N" THEN 30

50 REM-------IF YOU DON'T KNOW YOUR BLOOD
   TYPE

60 IF N$="N" THEN PRINT" WELL THEN HURRY AND
   FIND OUT. WE'LL BE WAITING FOR
   YOU":PRINT" WAITING STARTS NOW........":
   END

70 REM---------B$ IS USER INPUT
```

```
80 PRINT:INPUT"OK-WHAT IS IT-DON'T FORGET I
   NEED A LETTER (S) AND A SIGN (+) OR
   (-)";B$

90 REM---------BLOOD TYPE PROBABILITIES

100 REM---A+

110 IF B$="A+" THEN PRINT:PRINT" 38% OR 38
    OUT OF EVERY 100 PEOPLE HAVE YOUR BLOOD
    TYPE AND IN CASE OF PERSONAL PERIL REST
    ASSURED YOU HAVE MANY DONORS":END

REM---O+

130 IF B$="O+"PRINT:PRINT"36% OR 36 OF EVERY
    100 PEOPLE HAVE YOUR BLOOD TYPE--NO
    SWEAT FOR YOU IN CASE YOU NEED A QUICK
    TRANSFUSION!!!!!!!":END

140 REM---B+
```

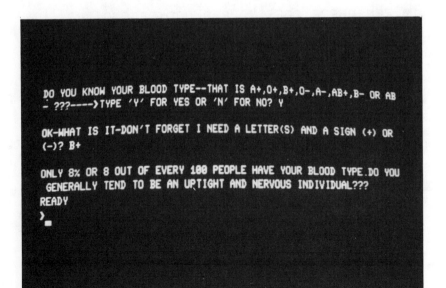

```
150 IF B$="B+"PRINT:PRINT" ONLY 8% OR 8 OUT
    OF EVERY 100 PEOPLE HAVE YOUR BLOOD
    TYPE. DO YOU GENERALLY TEND TO BE AN
    UPTIGHT AND NERVOUS INDIVIDUAL???":END

160 REM--- O- OR A-

170 IF B$="O-" OR B$="A-" THEN PRINT:PRINT"
    DON'T GET TOO UPSET BUT ONLY 6% OR 6 OUT
    OF EVERY 100 PEOPLE HAVE YOUR BLOOD
    TYPE. HAVE YOU EVER MADE A SERIOUS
    EFFORT TO LOCATE SOME OF THESE
    INDIVIDUALS----IF YOU COULD FIND
    THEM???":END

180 REM---AB+

190 IF B$="AB+"PRINT:PRINT"ONLY 3.5% OR
    ABOUT 3-4 OUT OF EVERY 100 PEOPLE HAVE
    YOUR BLOOD TYPE. I KNOW YOU MUST FEEL
    SORT OF RARE BUT HAVE YOU EVER THOUGHT
    OF GETTING HOLD OF SOME OF THEM AND
    STARTING YOUR OWN BLOOD BANK???":END
```

```
DO YOU KNOW YOUR BLOOD TYPE--THAT IS A+,O+,B+,O-,A-,AB+,B- OR AB
- ???---->TYPE 'Y' FOR YES OR 'N' FOR NO? Y

OK-WHAT IS IT-DON'T FORGET I NEED A LETTER(S) AND A SIGN (+) OR
(-)? AB+

ONLY 3.5% OR ABOUT 3-4 OUT OF EVERY 100 PEOPLE HAVE YOUR
BLOOD TYPE. I KNOW YOU MUST FEEL SORT OF RARE BUT HAVE YOU EVER
THOUGHT OF GETTING A HOLD OF SOME OF THEM AND STARTING YOUR OWN
BLOOD BANK???
READY
>
```

```
200 REM---B-

210 IF B$="B-"THEN PRINT:PRINT" NOW I DON'T
    MEAN TO ALARM YOU BUT I GUESS YOU KNOW
    THAT ONLY 2% OR 2 OUT OF EVERY 100
    PEOPLE HAVE YOUR BLOOD TYPE.LOOK ON THE
    BRIGHTER SIDE; IT'S BETTER THAN BEING IN
    THE 1% CATEGORY":END

220 REM--- AB-

230 IF B$="AB-" THEN PRINT:PRINT" SINCE ONLY
    .5% OR 1/2 OF A PERSON OUT OF EVERY 100
    PEOPLE HAS YOUR BLOOD TYPE HAVE YOU
    SERIOUSLY CONSIDERED DOING YOUR OWN
    TRANSFUSION ON YOURSELF EVERY SO OFTEN
    AND SAVING IT IN THE ICE BOX---JUST IN
    CASE???":END

240 REM-------NONHUMAN BLOOD POSSIBILITY

250 PRINT"I DON'T RECOGNIZE THAT STRANGE
    STRAND-ARE YOU SURE IT'S HUMAN?--- TRY
    AGAIN":GOTO80
```

Compound Interest

```
10 REM-- COMPOUND INTEREST

20 REM---AN EXAMPLE

30 CLS:PRINT"IT'S NICE TO KNOW HOW MUCH
   MONEY YOU WILL EARN OVER A PERIOD OF TIME
   IF YOU INVESTED IT SOMEWHERE"

40 PRINT:PRINT"FOR EXAMPLE-IF YOU LEFT
   $500.00 IN A SAVINGS ACCOUNT FOR FIVE
   YEARS AT 6% COMPOUND ANNUAL INTEREST YOUR
   NEW AMOUNT WOULD BE "

50 REM---A  REPRESENTS ACCUMULATED AMOUNT

60 REM--- WE'LL LOOK AT THIS FORMULA AGAIN
```

```
70 A=500*(1+.06) ^ 5

80 REM-----A ROUNDING-OFF FORMULA

90 A=INT((A+.005)*100)/100

100 REM-----------------------------

110 INPUT"PRESS 'S' TO SEE";S$

120 IF S$<>"S"THEN 640
130 PRINT"$" A

140 PRINT:PRINT"INTEREST EARNED YOU "A-500 "
    NOT BAD--EH?"

150 REM----------------------------

160 INPUT" TYPE 'C' TO CONTINUE";C$

170 IF C$<>"C"THEN 640
```

```
IT'S NICE TO KNOW HOW MUCH MONEY YOU WILL EARN OVER A PERIOD OF
TIME IF YOU INVESTED IT SOMEWHERE

FOR EXAMPLE-IF YOU LEFT $500.00 IN A SAVINGS ACCOUNT FOR FIVE
YEARS AT 6% COMPOUND ANNUAL INTEREST YOUR NEW AMOUNT WOULD BE
PRESS 'S' TO SEE? S
$ 669.11

INTEREST EARNED YOU  169.11  NOT BAD--EH?
TYPE 'C' TO CONTINUE?
```

```
180 REM--- ANOTHER EXAMPLE

190 CLS:PRINT" COMPOUND INTEREST IS INTEREST
    ON YOUR ORIGINAL AMOUNT AS WELL AS THE
    INTEREST THIS AMOUNT IS ACCUMULATING.IT
    CAN BE FIGURED ON A DAILY,MONTHLY, OR
    YEARLY BASIS"

200 INPUT"TYPE 'R' IF YOU ARE INTERESTED IN
    MORE INTEREST INFO";R$

210 IF R$<>"R"THEN 640

220 REM---------------------------

230 CLS:PRINT"LET'S SAY YOU LEFT $50.00 IN
    THE BANK AT 8% COMPOUNDED A DAY FOR 30
    DAYS. HERE'S WHAT YOU'LL SEE GROWING

240 INPUT" TYPE 'G' FOR GO";G$

250 IF G$<>"G"THEN 640

260 REM---BEGIN LOOP

270 FORN=1 TO30

280 PRINT:PRINT"AT THE END OF DAY "N " YOUR
    AMOUNT WILL BE

290 REM------- N=NUMBER OF TIMES INTEREST IS
    COMPOUNDED IN A YEAR

300 REM------- T=NUMBER OF YEARS

310 T=.08

320 A=50*(1+.08/N)^(N*T)

330 PRINT:PRINT "$"A

340 FORY=1 TO 500:NEXT Y
```

```
350 NEXT N

360 REM---END LOOP

370 A=INT((A+.005)*100)/100

380 PRINT:PRINT" TO THE NEAREST CENT IT
    IS----→$"A

390 REM------------------------

400 PRINT:PRINT"TYPE 'T' IF YOU WANT TO TRY
    ONE"

410 INPUT T$

420 IF T$<>"T"THEN 640

430 REM------TIME FOR YOU TO DO ONE

440 CLS:PRINT"INTEREST CAN BE COMPOUNDED
    ANNUALLY (1), QUARTERLY (4), TWICE A
    YEAR (2), BY THE DAY (360) ETC"
```

```
INTEREST CAN BE COMPOUNDED ANNUALLY (1),QUARTERLY (4),TWICE A
YEAR (2), BY THE DAY (360) ETC
 TYPE IN THE NUMBER OF TIMES THAT YOU WANT YOUR INTEREST
COMPOUNDED IN A YEAR? 4

 TYPE IN YOUR INVESTMENT DOLLARS- FOR EXAMPLE 10 OR 349.90 OR 50
000 OR 34.56 ETC? 1000

NOW FOR HOW MANY YEARS WOULD YOU LIKE IT COMPOUNDED 1,3,4,6.5,10
ETC)? 5

 WHAT IS YOUR INTEREST RATE--.05,.10,.08,.234,ETC? .06

 NOW STAND BACK I'M NUMBER CRUNCHING AND IT CAN BE QUITE MESSY
AT TIMES
```

```
450 INPUT" TYPE IN THE NUMBER OF TIMES THAT
    YOU WANT YOUR INTEREST COMPOUNDED IN A
    YEAR";N

460 PRINT

470 REM-------P REPRESENTS THE PRINCIPAL
    AMOUNT

480 INPUT" TYPE IN YOUR INVESTMENT DOLLARS-
    FOR EXAMPLE 10 OR 349.90 OR 50000 OR
    34.56 ETC";P

490 REM-------T REPRESENTS THE TIME IN YEARS

500 PRINT:INPUT"NOW FOR HOW MANY YEARS WOULD
    YOU LIKE IT COMPOUNDED (.5,1,3,4,6.5,10
    ETC);T

510 REM-------R REPRESENTS INTEREST RATE

520 PRINT:INPUT" WHAT IS YOUR INTEREST
    RATE--.05,.10,.08,.234,ETC";R

530 REM----------------------------

540 PRINT: PRINT" NOW STAND BACK I'M NUMBER
    CRUNCHING AND IT CAN BE QUITE MESSY AT
    TIMES"

550 REM----LOOP TO SLOW THINGS DOWN

560 FOR K=1 TO 2000:NEXT K :CLS

570 A=P*(1+R/N) ^ (N*T)

580 A=INT((A+.005)*100)/100

590 REM----- YOUR RESULTS

600 PRINT:PRINT" YOUR TOTAL AMOUNT IS $"A "
    AND YOU HAVE EARNED " A-P " IN INTEREST"
```

```
610 REM----------------------

620 PRINT:INPUT"TYPE 'A' IF YOU WOULD LIKE
    TO DO ANOTHER OR 'E' TO END"; A$

630 IF A$="A"THEN 440

640 CLS:PRINT"I HAD ENOUGH FOR NOW--- THANK
    YOU!!!!!"
```

QUICK SPELLER

```
10 REM RECALL TIME

20 REM-----PURPOSE

30 CLS:PRINT"I WILL QUICKLY FLASH A WORD ON
   THE CRT.YOU MUST CORRECTLY SPELL IT BACK
   TO ME. YOU CAN CHOOSE AT MOST FIVE
   WORDS."
```

I WILL QUICKLY FLASH A WORD ON THE CRT. YOU MUST CORRECTLY SPELL
IT BACK TO ME. YOU CAN CHOOSE AT MOST FIVE WORDS

TYPE 'R' WHEN YOU ARE READY?

```
40  PRINT:INPUT"TYPE 'R' WHEN YOU ARE
    READY";R$

50  IF R$<>"R"THEN 40

60  REM-------READING THE 5 WORDS--BEGIN LOOP

70  FORI= 1 TO 5

80  REM-------W$ IS AN ARRAY HOLDING FIVE
    WORDS

90    READ W$(I)

100   CLS

110   PRINT:PRINT:PRINT:PRINT

120 REM--------PRINTING EACH WORD

130   PRINT"                   " W$(I)

140 REM---SLOWING DOWN OUTPUT

150   FOR X= 1 TO 100:NEXT X:CLS
```

```
160 REM---Y$ REPRESENTS USER INPUT

170   INPUT " YOUR SPELLING PLEASE ";Y$

180 REM--------IF RIGHT

190   IF W$(I)=Y$ THEN 250

200 REM-----------IF WRONG

210   PRINT:PRINT" NOT RIGHT--TRY AGAIN"

220   FOR V=1 TO 200:NEXT V

230 GOTO 130

240 REM----------------

250   CLS:PRINT " THAT'S VERY GOOD"

260 REM-------------CHECK FOR LAST WORD

270   IF I=5 THEN 320

280 REM-----GO AGAIN???
```

```
290    INPUT" ENTER THE LETTER 'A' IF YOU
       WANT ANOTHER OR 'N' FOR END";A$

300    IF A$="A" THEN NEXT I

310 REM---END LOOP

320 PRINT " KEEP THE FAITH AND CATCH YOU
    LATER"

330 REM---------------THE FIVE WORDS

340    DATA CHIP,OUTPUT,TERMINAL,PRINTER,
    MICROCOMPUTER
```

Chapter 9

A LOOK AT LOGO, PASCAL, AND PILOT

The Other Languages

BASIC is a very popular programming language used in both education and noneducation circles. However, some purists contend that BASIC is not the language to learn if one wants to study programming. They say that Pascal is more suitable since its very structure enables one to develop sound programming techniques and habits.

Logo is another language that fosters such an approach and even offers more. Its creators claim that it was developed as a reflection of our thinking processes and as a result it places emphasis on the user's ability to think through a problem. And then there's PILOT. It is best suited to allow the user to interact with the computer in a question-and-answer manner.

BASIC, Logo, Pascal, and PILOT are the predominant programming languages being used in the schools today. Since we already know what BASIC is all about let's take a quick look at some of the features of the other three.

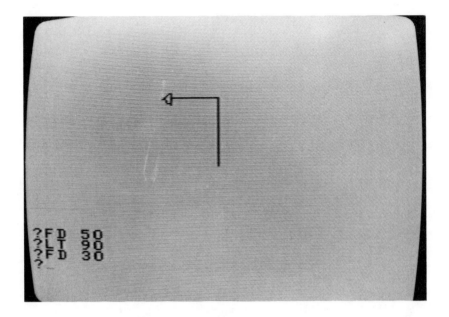

Logo

One frequently employed feature of Logo (from the Greek meaning *reason*) is its turtle graphics. Here students learn programming by commanding a small triangular figure named a turtle to move on the screen. By choosing from a list of reserved words (TI Logo is demonstrated here), users can interact with their turtle and get it to move in various directions creating their own graphic designs. Some of these commands are:

FD ————— FORWARD (spaces)

BK ————— BACK (spaces)

LT ————— LEFT TURN (angle)

RT ————— RIGHT TURN (angle)

PU ————— PEN UP (no draw)

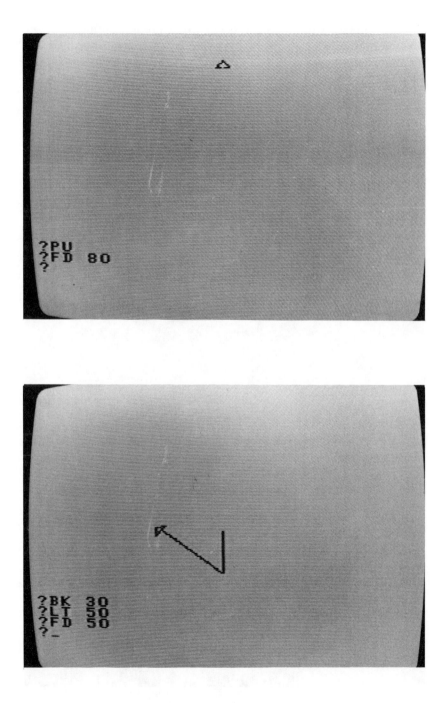

Students use these commands in a program they define by a user name. The following shows such a program or procedure called TO TRI. Once defined it can be used at any time by just calling or naming TRI:

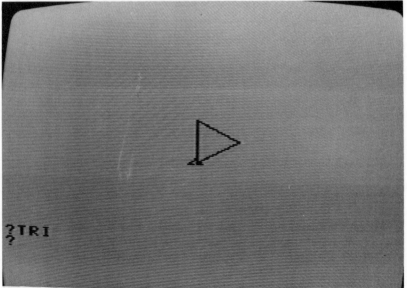

The REPEAT command saves some time and labor:

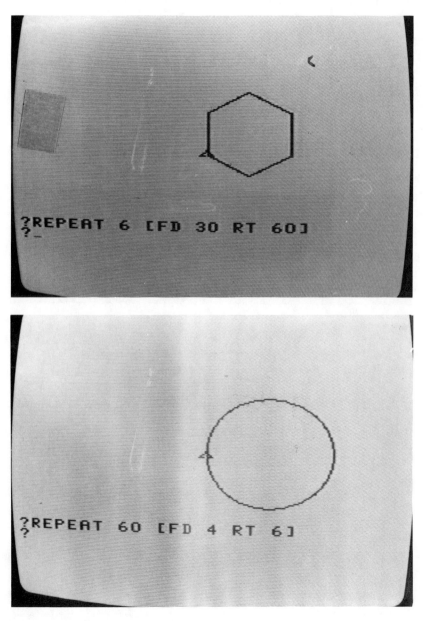

Once a procedure has been defined it can be used within itself or in another procedure by just naming it. This illustrates Logo's recursive properties. For example, the TO BOX program contains the BOX procedure itself and consequently calls FD 30 and RT 90 repeatedly until stopped by the user:

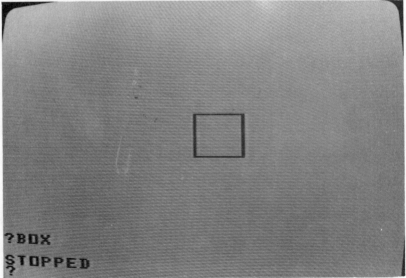

The ability to create in Logo a procedure within a procedure makes it expansive in its possibilities.

The BOX procedure can also contain variables that allow the student to input values for SIDE and ANGLE:

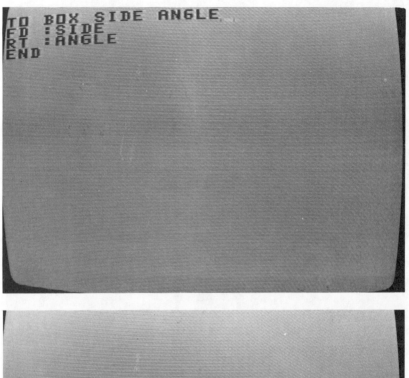

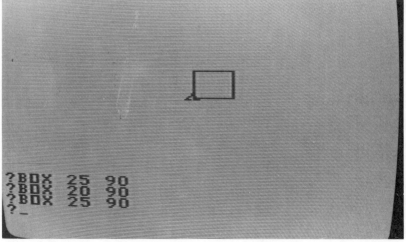

Of course, there is an almost limitless source of other possibilities:

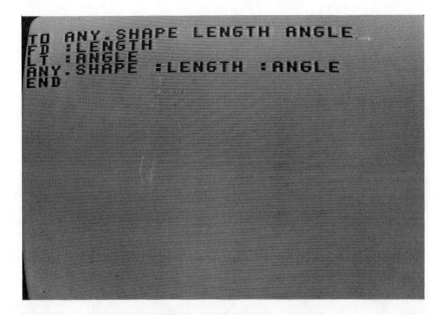

```
TO ANY.SHAPE LENGTH ANGLE
FD :LENGTH
LT :ANGLE
ANY.SHAPE :LENGTH :ANGLE
END
```

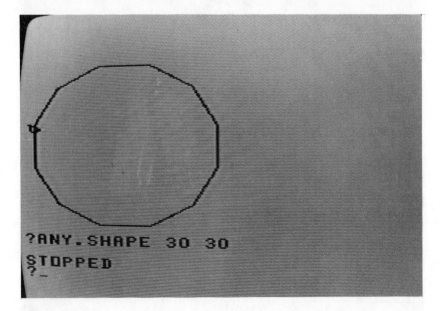

```
?ANY.SHAPE 30 30
STOPPED
?_
```

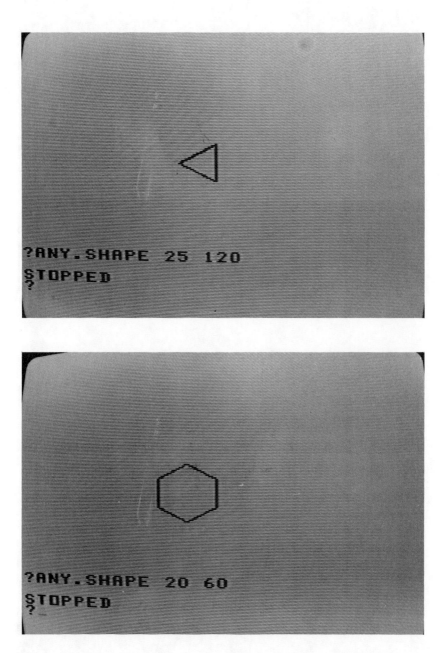

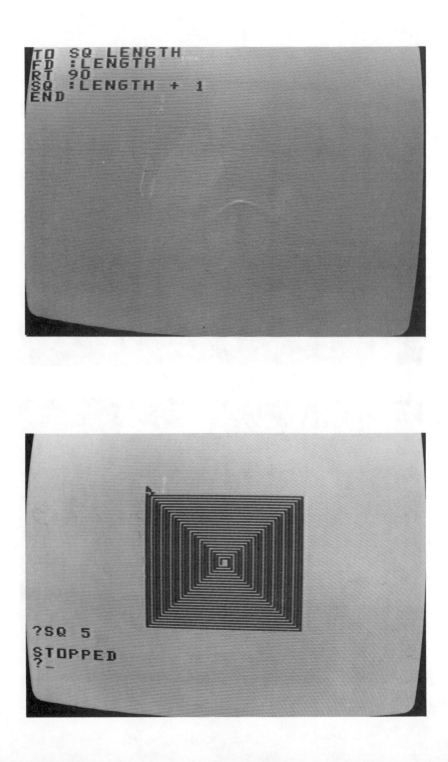

In addition to its popular graphic capabilities, Logo can be used to create lists of numbers, letters, words, or other lists. Brackets are used to contain the elements of a list and reserved words are employed to manipulate these elements. The name of each list shown below comes after the brackets:

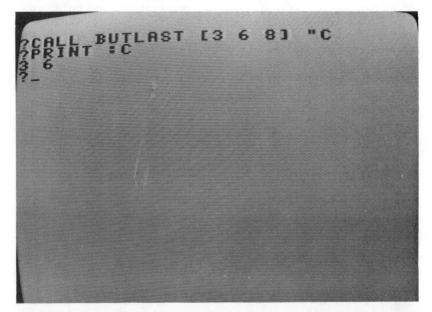

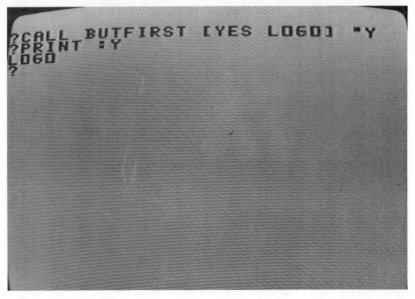

Since the list processing of Logo can range from the simple (see photos) to the very complex, the turtle graphics of Logo will probably appeal to most students. Practical applications in the list processing aspects of Logo need to be developed better if all students are to benefit from Logo's full features.

Computation and assignment statements are also part of Logo:

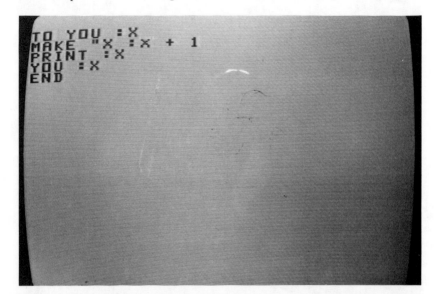

Logo has a definite place in the school curriculum as a language that stresses problem-solving behavior. Its user-friendliness along with its underlining theme of guiding the learner through his thinking processes are its greatest assets.

Pascal

The importance of Pascal (after the philosopher Blaise Pascal: 1623–1662) in the schools is that it forces one to use sound programming techniques. This is not usually the case when coding in unstructured BASIC—it is very easy to write a lengthy program in this language and later find yourself unable to follow your own logic. This is not meant to happen when working in Pascal.

Pascal imposes structure on those who use it. For example, when one begins to code in Pascal certain steps and rules must be followed. The program must first be named. Variables, if they are used, need to be defined according to type: integer or real. Programs must then be enclosed with **BEGIN/END** statements and proper use of periods, colons, commas, and semicolons must be followed.

In the case of any program, what finally emerges in Pascal is code that is orderly and readable. Here is a simple example of Pascal for calculating distance given rate and time:

```
PROGRAM DISTANCE:

VAR RATE        :REAL;

    TIME        :REAL;

    DIST        :REAL;

BEGIN

    RATE:=20;

    TIME:=5.5;

    DIST:=RATE*TIME

WRITELN('DISTANCE=',DIST:8:2);

END.
```

Note that Pascal does not contain line numbers. The programmer must code in a top-down fashion which means creating blocks of programs each with a purpose. This is not so in BASIC where the use of GOTOs and GOSUBs can send the reader to any line in the program. The resultant code can become quite unmanageable. Of course, BASIC can be coded in a block-type and top-down fashion but one must use a high degree of self-discipline to do so.

The formal discipline required to program in Pascal makes it a language suitable for the high school years. Its greatest asset as a programming language is its emphasis on developing sound computer science skills. This trait is especially useful when coding programs where structure is a desirable goal.

PILOT

PILOT (PROGRAMMING, INQUIRY, LEARNING OR TEACHING) provides the user with a simple approach to programming. While other language commands can be esoteric, PILOT's single letter commands make it straightforward and understandable for the first-time user. PILOT was originally developed for a single purpose: namely, for the creation of test questions by teachers. Consequently, it is a very efficient language in an environment for handling text.

Here are some single-letter commands, and how each is used. For comparison, the BASIC equivalent command is in parentheses on the right:

    T: displays output on screen (PRINT)
    A: wait for user response (INPUT)
    M: match input with answer (none)
    R: nonexecutable comment (REM)
    E: end program or module (END)

Some versions of PILOT are also capable of graphics and sound which can be used to enhance the interactive nature of the program. The following is an example of a PILOT program:

```
10 R:TEST TIME

20 T:WHAT IS YOUR NAME?
```

```
30  A:$NAME

40  T:WHO DISCOVERED AMERICA NAME$

50  A:$A

60  M:COLUMBUS/CHRISTOPHER COLUMBUS/
    C.COLUMBUS

70  TY:GOOD JOB $NAME

80  TN:SORRY $NAME BUT $A IS NOT RIGHT.YOU
    NEED TO STUDY MORE

90  E:
```

Note that in line 60 user response is matched against any three correct answers. If any one of the three is correct then line 70 is executed. If none are correct then 80 is done.

PILOT is not sophisticated enough to perform more than simple math. As a result, it cannot compete with BASIC or Pascal in this area. However, it is an ideal language for the beginner since it possesses the logical and problem-solving principles of a programming language while being enjoyable to use.

WHY ANY ONE??????????

All students should be given the opportunity to learn a programming language as part of their regular curriculum. This is not because we want to train them to be our future programmers.

The main reason is the control it will give students in an environment where conformity to rules and procedures is an important goal that nonetheless can be stifling to intellectual growth and expression. Problem solving, logical thinking, and creativity are the skills that will develop, to varying degrees, in those who take on the challenge of being in charge. Students will be given the opportunity to do their own thing for a change. Involved in the whole process will be a sense of excitement and fun—ingredients that should be part of the learning process but many times are missing in the classroom.

WHICH ONE AND WHEN???????????

There is not, and probably will not be, the perfect programming language for everyone to learn. As we have seen, each language has a definite purpose. Given the human condition, it will probably be impossible to invent the programming language that will meet everyone's needs and interests.

If it is possible, all four programming languages should be available in a school. Each has features that can be matched with a student's needs and abilities. Let's look at a suggested scope and sequence outline for these four languages. But before we do, some educators might be scratching their heads over how all four programming languages can be part of a required curriculum in an already crowded student and teacher schedule. This is possible because as students learn their basic reading, math, or social studies skills at the computer (remember, this was discussed in Chapter 4) there should be more time to do other things.

All students as early as the primary years (grades K-3) might start off with Logo because of its graphic appeal, friendly guiding nature, and structured design.   Then somewhere in the middle grades (4th, 5th, and 6th) some of these students who show ability and interest in Logo can pursue it further and/or get into the area of simple list processing. Other students at this point who still show interest, but not with list processing, could continue with turtle graphics or go into PI-LOT. This language possesses some fine features while remaining fairly easy to use.

And at this time or even earlier there will be some students who will show no desire, ability, or interest in learning a programming language. They, of course, should be given the opportunity to pursue nonprogramming software that involves tapping problem solving and creative skills.

As we follow these students through the grades, the more able and interested who are about in junior high now (7th–8th grades) should start some BASIC. Some of our programming purists might quake at their terminals at such a thought but, let's face it, BASIC is a language with many fine features. It's interactive and can do scientific as well as nonscientific programming. And it is essentially an easy language that is used widely. BASIC is and will probably always be a language to consider because of its availability, popularity, and versatility. The nonacademic track students can continue with Logo, PILOT, or some other type of nonprogramming problem-solving activities.

In the high school years the academic track computer science student can finish BASIC in grade 9 and then go into Pascal for the remainder of high school. For the other students who will probably not major in the field, BASIC will probably be best for them for the rest of the high school years. Others who haven't had any programming, or had a little of Logo in the early grades may try some simple commands in BASIC, PILOT or Logo.

Student → GRADE ↓	Basic	General	Academic
K-3	Logo	Logo	Logo
4-6	Logo/NON-PROGRAMMING ACTIVITIES	Logo/PILOT	Logo
7-8	"	"	BASIC
9-12	Logo/PILOT/ BASIC	BASIC	Pascal

In addition to these four languages there are the application languages of COBOL and RPG that are taught in the business departments of some schools. Those students who have had some experience in the early grades with Logo, PILOT, or BASIC might find learning another language a little easier.

As students progress from one language to another they will have to adjust to the style and commands of each language. Some confusion will exist in the beginning but eventually such an experience should help them assimilate each new language and appreciate the uniqueness of each.

Some Words of Caution

Before any school district implements into their program any one or all of these languages they must have the qualified and interested personnel who will do the teaching. They should also have a course outline or syllabus for each programming language taught in each grade. The rationale is simple. Too often in education potentially sound programs have gone the way of the dust collector: the closet.

This happens mainly whenever teachers are not well informed on a consistent basis as to what is expected of them. The teacher has enough to do in the course of a day and should not be expected to implement district curriculum that is sketchy and ambiguous.

In many cases we find students left on their own at the computer to do some discovery learning because teachers themselves don't know what is expected of them. Teachers need structure from "above" to get them started and that will stay with them for some time. Once this is accomplished each teacher should be able to take control of the situation and do a fine job. However, in the beginning there must be careful planning for what the needs are and how they should be met. Evaluation of the process should be ongoing. The final results will prove beneficial for both student achievement and teacher effectiveness.

Chapter 10

CONCLUSION—AN EXCITING FUTURE

THE FUTURE

A school district that has long-range plans for including computers into its curriculum has already planted the necessary seeds for the future. The goal of the first nine chapters of this book was to help educators get started in this direction.

Once a district begins to implement these plans it will encounter many exciting and evolving opportunities for growth. The only obstacles are a lack of daring, sporadic efforts, and poor leadership.

ARTIFICIAL INTELLIGENCE

The computers of the future are currently being developed and tested. Some of them are being designed to think and reason as humans. This holds an exciting promise for educators teaching problem-solving skills, perhaps the most difficult area. Of course, no computer can ever assume all the human qualities since no one probably ever will grasp and understand the qualities of being human.

Telecommunications

Connecting a micro to a phone opens the school doors to many possibilities. Homebound students can do their assignments at their computer and receive feedback from the one at school.

Those students who qualify can receive college credit for courses while at home or at school.

Students with conflicting schedules may be able to take their conflict courses at another school in or outside the district. Data bases can also be accessed. Current news, encyclopedias, business reports, and bulletin boards are just some of the sources available within minutes inside the classroom while at the keyboard.

The school of the future as a focal point of information and services for its teachers and students will be an exciting place to be.

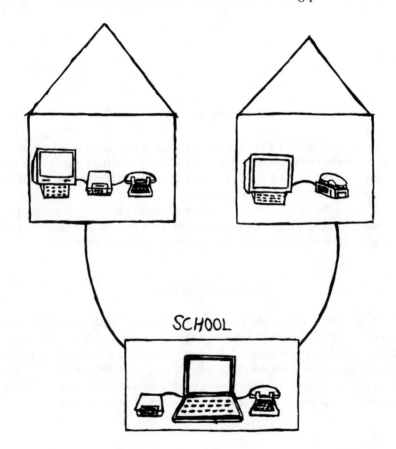

SCHOOL

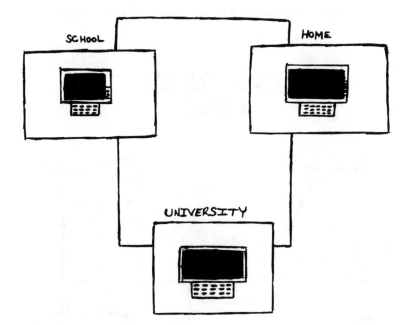

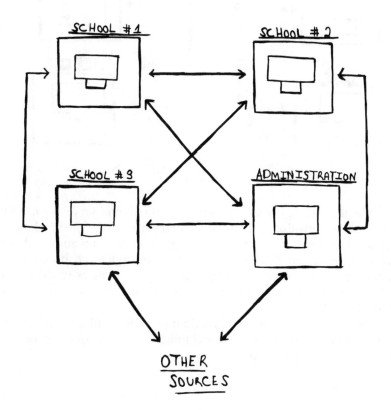

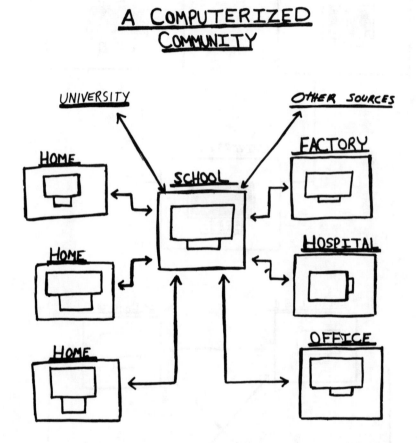

ROBOTICS

The increasing use of robots in industry should serve as a call for educators to introduce "them" into the curriculum. On the elementary level, students can use simple programming commands to direct a robot's movement. On the junior and senior high level, more sophisticated programming to move the robot can be done as students also learn the basic concepts of machines and their uses (La Von Blaesi & Maness, 1984).

The use of robots in the classroom provides students with an excellent opportunity to perform manipulative endeavors and receive instant feedback at the same time.

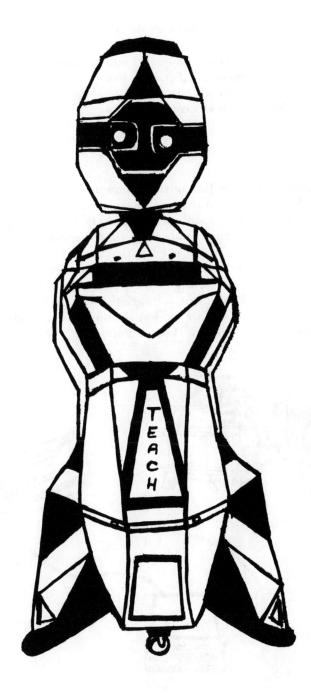

Videodisks and VCRs

Videodisks and VCRs can be tied into computers to provide students with interactive self-paced instruction (Thorkildsen & Friedman, 1984). Students control the motion of the video and respond to video questions by computer input.

Things to Consider

Although the ramifications of computer education hold high promise for students and teachers, there are concerns and cautions. The availability of quality software to make the hardware operational must always be of prime concern to the educator. Such software should present subject matter in a way that was previously impossible. It should primarily motivate and stimulate students to learn, the most difficult task facing most teachers in the classroom today.

Reasonably priced quality software that can be easily duplicated or made available in quantity without violating any copyrights should be arranged with publishers. If this is impossible, then the growth of

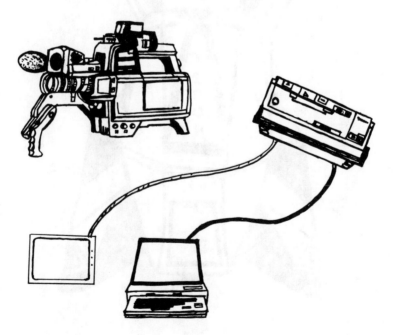

computer education will be stifled as neither schools nor publishers will benefit.

Educators must serve as role models for their students regarding copying programs illegally or breaking into restricted data bases. Such behavior might seem expeditious or exciting at the time but it will only lead to eventual problems.

Machines can only do so much and hardware breakdowns will be inevitable. Provisions in school budgets must be made to handle maintenance problems when the warranty expires.

Finally, both teachers and students should not expect instant miracles. As with any revolutionary idea, time, persistence, and hard work are the ingredients needed to reap the eventual rewards. What is hoped to emerge is the image of a professional, respected by all, and in charge of a situation which provides a stimulating learning environment for his students.

APPENDIX A—ANSWER KEY

Chapter 6

Suggested Answer Key

These are suggested answers. In some cases you may have your own that will provide similar results.

For PRINT statement

1. C

2.

```
PRINT "FAR              FARTHER              FARTHEST"
         :
```

3.

```
10 PRINT "TRY              TRY"

20 PRINT "TO               TO"

30 PRINT "REMEMBER         FORGET"
```

4.

```
10 PRINT"              X"

20 PRINT"        X        X"

30 PRINT"        X        X"

40 PRINT"        X        X"

50 PRINT"          XXX"

60 PRINT"          XXX"
```

5.

```
LAST NAME, FIRST NAME
```

6. Can't squeeze a line number between lines 3 and 4!

7. Quotes must be paired. The extra third quote will create a problem.

```
30 PRINT " " ".
```

For GOTO statement

1.

```
10 PRINT "Your name goes here"

20 CLS

30 GOTO 10
```

2. Program is "stuck" at line 20.

```
FREEZE - THIS IS A STICK-UP.
```

3.

```
40 GOTO 70
```

4.

```
50 GOTO 20
```

5. C

For numeric variables, LET statement, and arithmetic functions

1.

```
10 A = 5

20 B = 5

30 PRINT " 5 TIMES 5 = "A*B

40 PRINT " 5 DIVIDED BY 5 = "A/B

50 PRINT " 5 MINUS 5 = "A-B
```

2.

```
10 A = 5

20 B = 2

30 C = 3

40 PRINT A, A*B, A*C
```

3.

```
PRINT 23.59-8+42*6/12-7*8.2^2
```

4. C

5.

```
10 SUE = 15

20 BOB =  3
```

For INPUT statement, string, and numeric variables

1.

```
10 INPUT "TYPE IN YOUR FRIEND'S NAME AND HIS
   AGE"; N$,A

20 PRINT " MY FRIEND IS " N$ " AND HE IS "A"
   YEARS OLD"
```

2.

```
10 INPUT "TYPE IN TWO NUMBERS AND I WILL ADD
   THEM"; A,B
```

3. C

4.

```
10 INPUT "WHAT IS THE BASE OF YOUR
   TRIANGLE"; B

20 INPUT "WHAT IS THE HEIGHT OF YOUR
   TRIANGLE"; H

30 PRINT "THE BASE IS " B

40 PRINT "THE HEIGHT IS " H

50 PRINT "THE AREA OF YOUR TRIANGLE IS "
   .5*B*H
```

5.

```
10 INPUT "TYPE IN ANY TWO NUMBERS AND I WILL
   DIVIDE AND SUBTRACT THEM"; Q,F

20 PRINT "THEIR QUOTIENT IS " Q/F

30 PRINT "THEIR DIFFERENCE IS "Q-F
```

For IF-THEN statement

1.

```
15 IF N$>M
```

2.

```
30 IF A<B THEN PRINT " YOUR HIGHER NUMBER IS
   " B :END
```

```
40 PRINT "YOUR HIGHER NUMBER IS " A
```

3. In line 30 if your input number is not equal (<>) to 8 then line 60 is executed. If it is 8 then it sends you back to line 20 (40-50-20).

4.

```
05 L$ = "A BULL MOOSE"
```

```
10 G$ = "A NEWSPAPER"
```

```
20 B$ = "A BLUSHING ZEBRA"
```

```
25 INPUT" WHAT IS BLACK, WHITE AND RED ALL
   OVER"; M$
```

```
30 IF B$ = M$ THEN PRINT "YOU'RE
   RIGHT  "B$:END
```

```
35 PRINT "NOPE: TRY AGAIN"
```

```
40 GOTO 25
```

For counting assignment statements

1.

```
45 IF G = 100 THEN END
```

2. B

3.

```
10 INPUT "WHAT IS YOUR LAST NUMBER"; L

20 C=C+1

30 IF L=C THEN PRINT "YOUR LAST NUMBER AND
   THE COUNTER ARE BOTH " L:END

40 GOTO 20
```

4.

```
05 N= 0:C=0

10 N= N+.05

20 C=C+1

30 PRINT "DAY" C "EQUALS" N

40 IF C = 30 THEN END

50 GOTO 10
```

For FOR-NEXT loop

1. C

2.

```
10 FOR S = 0 TO 100 STEP 5

20 PRINT S;

30 NEXT S
```

3.

```
20 FOR X = 150 TO 1 STEP-1
```

4. The value of X in line 30 will always be 0.

5.

```
15 INPUT "HOW HIGH DO YOU WANT YOUR NUMBER-
   THE HIGHER THE SLOWER"; H

40 FOR Y = 1 TO H : NEXT Y
```

CHAPTER 7

Suggested Answer Key

For RND function

1. **B**

2.

```
10 N=RND(50)

20 T=RND(50)
```

3.

```
15 N=RND(25)

30 IF T<N THEN INPUT "TOO LOW-TRY AGAIN"; T:
   C=C+1: GO TO 30

40 IF T>N THEN INPUT "TOO HIGH-GO AGAIN"; T:
   C=C+1: GO TO 30

55 PRINT "IT ONLY TOOK YOU" C "TRIES"
```

4. The value of X could be greater than the value of Y causing an error.

5.

```
50 IF D1=6 AND D2=6 PRINT "WHOOPS---TWO
   SIXES YOU LOSE!!":END
```

For READ and DATA statements

1.

```
10 READ N$,A

20 PRINT N$,D

30 DATA MARY IS,32
```

2. A

3. Will get an error. Need a NEXT statement to go with line 10.

4.

```
10 READ P$

15 IF P$="END" THEN END

20 PRINT P$

30 DATA CAT, DOG, FISH, BIRD, FROG, BULL
   MOOSE, END

40 GOTO 10
```

5. D

For assignment statements

1.

```
20 T=1: REM IF T=0 THE PRODUCT WILL BE 0

50 T=T*N

100 PRINT "THAT'S MULTIPLICATION! - YOUR
    FINAL PRODUCT IS "T
```

2. If your sum is equal to or greater than 1000 the program will end.
    Line 30 keeps track of your sum (J).
3. C

For DIM statement

1. **B**
2.

```
15 DIM L(50)

30 FORY=1 TO 50
```

3.

```
30 C(X)=T

40 G(X)=S
```

For GOSUB and RETURN statements

1.

```
30 GOSUB 60

35 END
```

2.

```
LAST NAME -

FIRST NAME -

MIDDLE NAME -

THAT'S IT FOLKS---THERE AIN't NO MORE
```

3.

```
HI THERE

GOOD
```

APPENDIX B—READINGS

Educators seeking out ideas for using computers in the classroom can get firsthand experience by visiting other schools and by attending workshops and meetings. When this is not feasible, the next best thing is to read microcomputer periodicals, from cover to cover if possible.

Such journals will contain a wide variety of references that could directly benefit you, and will also refer you to other contacts and sources of information. Below is a partial listing to get you started:

Classroom Computer Learning
19 Davis Drive
Belmont, CA 94002

The Computing Teacher
Department of Computer Science
University of Oregon
Eugene, OR 97403

Educational Computer
3199 De La Cruz
Santa Clara, CA 95050

Electronic Education
1311 Executive Center Drive
Suite 220
Tallahassee, FL 32301

Electronic Learning
730 Broadway
New York, NY 10003

Teaching and Computers
Scholastic, Inc.
730 Broadway
New York, NY 10003

TLC
P.O. Box 9159
Brea, CA 92621

T.H.E. Journal
P.O. Box 364
Arlington, MA 02174

REFERENCES

CHAPTER 1

Gallup, G. 15th Annual Gallup Poll of the Public's Attitudes toward the Public Schools. *Phi Delta Kappan,* September 1983, 65(1), 33-47.

Norris, C., & Lumsden, B. Functional distance and attitudes of educators toward computers. *Technological Horizons in Education (T.H.E.) Journal,* January 1984, 2(4), 129-132.

O'Hanian, S. Beware the rosy view. *Classroom Computer Learning,* October 1983, 4(3), 21-27.

Survey finds: Micro's greatest educational import is social. *Electronic Learning,* September 1983, 3(1), 18.

Walker, D. Reflections on the educational potential and limitations of microcomputers. *Phi Delta Kappan,* October 1983, 65(2), 103-107.

Zienta, P. B. F. Skinner: Computers can cure what's wrong in American education. *Info World,* February 6, 1984, 23-25.

CHAPTER 2

Coburn, P., et al. *Practical guide to computers in education.* Reading, MA: Addison-Wesley Publishing Co, 1982.

Cowan, L. *The illustrated computer dictionary and handbook.* San Jose, CA: Enhich/O'Haus, 1983.

Harvey, W. Voice synthesis: A new technology comes to school. *Electronic Learning,* October 1983, 68-73.

Johnson, J. Educator's lexicon of computerese. *Arithmetic Teacher,* February 1983, 46-49.

Metzius, R. *The PDK guide: An introduction to microcomputer literacy for educators.* Bloomington, IN: Phi Delta Kappa, 1983.

Skapura, R. A Nod to the novice #4: Peripherals: Part 2. *The Computer Teacher,* November 83, 11(4), 29-30.

CHAPTER 3

Part A

Fisher, G. The social effects of computers in education. *Electronic Learning,* March 1984, 3(6), 26-28.

Green, J. B.F. Skinner's technology of teaching. *Classroom Computer Learning,* January 1984, 4(7), 23-29.

Hill, S. The microcomputer in the instructional program. *Arithmetic Teacher,* February 1983, 30(6), 14-15, 54,55.

Kantowski, M. The microcomputer and problem solving. *Arithmetic Teacher,* February 1983, 30(6), 20-21, 58,59.

Lathrop, A. The terrible ten in educational programming. *Educational Computer Magazine,* September/October 1982, 2(5), 34.

Lathrop, A., & Goodson, B. *Courseware in the classroom.* Menlo Park, CA: Addison-Wesley Publishing Co., 1983.

Riordan, T. How to select software you can trust. *The Classroom Computer News,* 56-61.

The learning software awards. *Classroom Computer Learning,* January 1984, 4(6), 52-57.

Vaugn, L., & Jones, W. (Eds.). *Evaluation of educational software: A guide to guides.* Chelmsford, MA: The Northeast Regional Exchange Inc., 1983.

Part B

Lesson Plan Authors

I   Margaret Dizzley
    Bishopville Primary School
    P.O. Box 7
    Bishopville, SC 29010

II   Phillip M. Chewning, Principal
      Bishopville Primary School
      P.O. Box 7
      Bishopville, SC 29010

III   Patricia Frierson
      West Lee Elementary School
      Rt. 1
      Rembert, SC 29128

IV   Viola R. Edwards
      Latta High School
      N. Richardson Street
      Latta, SC 29565

V   Eileen M. Filyaw
      Lake City High School
      Matthews Road
      Lake City, SC 29560

VI   Betty F. Ramey
      Francis Marion College
      Florence, SC 29501

VII   Flora P. Jenkins
      Latta High School
      N. Richardson Street
      Latta, SC 29565

VIII Sharon S. Johnson
      Cheraw High School
      Highway #9 West
      Cheraw, SC 25520

IX   Herbert Ash, Principal
      Bennettsville Intermediate School
      Rt. 3, Box 3
      Bennettsville, SC 29512

X   Annie B. Crawford
      Cheraw High School
      Highway #9 West
      Cheraw, SC 25520

XI   Delphine A. Peterson
West Lee Elementary School
Rt. 1
Rembert, SC 29128

XII   Laura D. Fenters
Timmonsville High School
Market Street Extension
Timmonsville, SC 29161

XIII   Anthony C. Maffei
St. John's High School
Darlington, SC 29532

CHAPTER 4

Anderson, E. The amazing library computer. *Electronic Learning*, March 1983, 2(6), 68-71.

Badiali, B. Micros make time for readability. *Educational Computer*, September/October 1982, 2(5), 26,76.

Behrmann, J. Computers talk to the blind. *TLC The Educator's Guide To Personal Computing*, March 1984, 1(5), 28-29.

Bockman, F. Creating your own software with mini-authoring systems. *Electronic Learning*, March 1983, 2(6), 72-75.

Cohen, M. Educational software: A taste of what's available for social studies. *The Computing Teacher*, December 1982, 11-15.

Files, C. Computerized career guidance that works. *Electronic Learning*, September 1983, 3(1), 78-81.

Freeman, E. Special tools for special kids. *TLC The Educator's Guide to Personal Computing*, December 1983, 51-57.

Hannaford, A. Microcomputers in special education: Some new opportunities, some old problems. *The Computing Teacher*, February 1983, 11-17.

Hively, W. Putting the computer to work. *Electronic Education*, April 1984, 3(7), 42, 54.

Hunter, B. Powerful tools for your social studies classroom. *Classroom Computer Learning*, October 1983, 4(3), 50-57.

Kalkstein, P. Computers on the playing field. *Electronic Learning*, October 1983, 3(2), 89-92.

Knapp, L. Buyer's guide: Word processors. *Electronic Learning*, March 1984, 3(6), 66-68.

Krolick, B. Computer access for the visually impaired. *The Computing Teacher,* April 1984, 11(8), 48-50.

Marcus, A. Graphic design for computer graphics. *The Computing Teacher,* April 1984, 11(8), 59-61.

Pennington, J. Word processing and teacher evaluation. *Electronic Learning,* March 1984, 3(6), 66-68.

Piper, K. The electronic writing machine: Using word processors with students. *The Computing Teacher,* December/January 1983-84, 11(5), 82-83.

Rodenstein, J. Microcomputers in vocational education. *Electronic Learning,* March 1983, 2(6), 54-59.

Russell, S. Logo in special education. *Classroom Computer Learning,* October 1983, 4(3), 34-39.

Shatkin, L. The electronic counselor. *Electronic Learning,* September 1983, 3(1), 75-77.

Walker, D. Reflections on the educational potential and limitations of microcomputers. *Phi Delta Kappan,* October 1983, 103-107.

CHAPTER 9

Billstein, R. Turtle fever. *The Computing Teacher,* September 1983, 11(2), 34-36.

Bromley, J. Pascal in high school. *The Computer Teacher,* October 1983, 11(3), 64-67.

Bruey, A. Choosing the language that works for you. *Electronic Education,* April 1984, 3(7), 110, 38-39.

Cron, M. Trouble in Logoland. *TLC The Educator's Guide to Personal Computing,* December 1983, 1(2), 59-65.

Harvey, B. Why Logo. *BYTE,* August 1982.

Harvey, W. Which programming language is right for you? *Classroom Computer Learning,* April/May 1984, 4(9), 51-53.

Lough, T. Logo: Discovery learning with the classroom's newest pet. *Electronic Learning,* March 1983, 2(6), 49-53.

Nansen, C. Teaching Pascal: The first nine weeks. *Electronic Learning,* September 1983a, 3(1), 50-54.

Nansen, C. Teaching Pascal: The second nine weeks. *Electronic Learning,* October 1983b, 3(2), 58-64.

Papert, S. *Mindstorms.* New York: Basic Books, 1980.

PILOT vs. BASIC. *Classroom Computer Learning,* October 1983, 4(3), 65.

Prosen, T. A programming language for elementary students. Association for educational data system convention. Paper. Portland, OR, May 1983.

Slesnick, T. Who's Pascal and why is he messing up my curriculum? *Classroom Computer Learning,* November/December 1983, 4(4), 54-60.

Stavely, T. List processing in Logo. *The Computing Teacher,* December 1982, 43-47.

Tinker, B. Logo's limits: Or which language should we teach? *Microcomputer in Education-Innovation and Issues,* Technical Education Research Centers, Newsletter, 6(1).

Chapter 10

Beyers, C. Telephone gives drill new twist. *Electronic Education,* October 1983, 3(2), 52-53.

Blaesi, L., & Maness, M. Robots: An impact on education. *T.H.E. Journal,* March 1984, 11(6), 100-104.

Green. J. Artificial intelligence and the future. *Classroom Computer Learning,* January 1984, 4(6), 26-31.

Hannah, L., & Matus, C. Teaching ethics in the computer classroom. *Classroom Computer Learning,* April/May 1984, 4(9), 32-36.

Levin, W. Interactive video: The state-of-the-art teaching machine. *The Computing Teacher,* September 1983, 11(2), 11-17.

Marsh, G., & Spain, T. Robots in the classroom. *Electronic Learning,* March 1984, 48-53, 112.

Martin, W. Touring an informational wonderland. *Classroom Computer Learning,* February 1984, 4(7), 52-60.

Schure, A. New images. *T.H.E. Journal,* February 1984, 2(5), 75-78.

Slesnick, T. Robots and kids: Classroom encounters. *Classroom Computer Learning,* March 1984, 4(8), 54-59.

Thorkildsen, R., & Friedman, S. Videodisks in the classroom. *T.H.E. Journal,* April 1984, 11(7), 90-95.

INDEX